FED UP

What's gone wrong with our government and steps to fix it

LARRY MCCALL

WESTBOW
PRESS®
A DIVISION OF THOMAS NELSON
& ZONDERVAN

WestBow Press books may be ordered through booksellers or by contacting:

WestBow Press
A Division of Thomas Nelson & Zondervan
1663 Liberty Drive
Bloomington, IN 47403
www.westbowpress.com
844-714-3454

Scripture quotations marked (NLT) are taken from the Holy Bible, New Living Translation, copyright © 1996, 2004, 2007 by Tyndale House Foundation. Used by permission of Tyndale House Publishers, Inc., Carol Stream, Illinois 60188. All rights reserved.

ISBN: 978-1-6642-2083-6 (sc)
ISBN: 978-1-6642-2082-9 (hc)
ISBN: 978-1-6642-2084-3 (e)

Library of Congress Control Number: 2021901362

Print information available on the last page.

WestBow Press rev. date: 02/08/2021

DEDICATION

I am dedicating this book to my wonderful, beautiful, and Godly wife, Paula. The support during this process has been the breath that has given life to this endeavor.

CONTENTS

INTRODUCTION

Every year the number of regulations, dictates, rules, decrees, guidelines, statutes, laws, and bylaws in the United States grows by leaps and bounds. Now it seems we can't go a week without hearing a new story about someone being punished with fines or even jail time, for activities that would be encouraged in a free society. I have researched some situations that I want to share with you, the reader, as an introduction to this book.

1. Single mom faces possible jail time for selling $12 worth of ceviche to an undercover police officer.
   Mariza Ruelas had her day in court in early November. Her crime? She sold a $12 plate of ceviche, an authentic Mexican dish, to an undercover cop on Facebook.

2. Federal prosecutors threaten Aaron Swartz with a life-crushing sentence for downloading academic articles.
   On January 11th, 2013, Aaron Swartz ended his own life, concluding one of the biggest miscarriages of justice in contemporary history. In the months leading up to his suicide, Swartz had been embroiled in a legal battle with the federal government after prosecutors charged Swartz under the draconian Computer Fraud and Abuse Act. His crime? Downloading thousands of academic articles from the JSTOR database.
   The CFAA is a particularly cruel piece of legislation, as it carries severe mandatory minimum sentencing requirements, resulting in Swartz facing up to 35 years in prison for a nonviolent crime.
   Many legal observers at the time pointed out that had Swartz robbed a bank, aided al-Qaeda, or produced child pornography he would have faced a more lenient sentence.

3. Government claims ownership of all water, jails Oregon man for 30 days for collecting rainwater on his own property

   Way back in 2012 the libertarian blogosphere was abuzz over a gregarious case of local government tyranny out of Oregon. Gary Harrington was sentenced to send 30 days in jail for the crime of collecting rainwater using three reservoirs (ponds) on his property. Oregon law states that all water is a public resource, to be owned communally by the collective population of Oregon, and as such any attempts to obtain or store water must first begin with applying for the proper permits to do so. Yes, really!

4. Maryland church ordered to evict homeless people from its property or pay a $12,000 fine.

   No good deed goes unpunished in the Land of the Free.TM. In late 2016, Reverend Katie Grover was met with a $12,000 citation attached to the door of the Patapsco United Methodist Church in Dundalk, Maryland. The alleged crime was allowing several homeless people to sleep on the church's property in violation of the county regulation prohibiting "no permitted rooming and boarding."

   The church wasn't even letting the homeless sleep indoors, rather they were just allowing a few homeless people to sleep on some of the benches located in the church's yard.

5. San Antonio chef fined $2,000 for feeding homeless people.

   In early 2015, the chef and founder of the not-for-profit food truck Chow Train, Joan Cheever was cited by police officers for the outrageous crime of serving hot meals to the city's homeless population.

   The citation, which she received for transporting the food in a different vehicle than her licensed food truck, carries with it a fine totaling $2,000.

If these illustrations do not make your blood boil, I am sure you could find even more outrageous abuses of freedom for the people.

I am sure that many of you who picked up this book are thinking that our country, our republic is a mess and also feel powerless to do anything about it. We are busy trying to make a living and raising a family, thinking that I will just let those who are in high and powerful positions to deal with it and hope that everything will be okay in the long run.

I am amazed how many good and righteous people we send to Washington or even to our state capitals who we think will get the job done but then end up the same as others we have sent because the glitz of money and power becomes too great of a temptation.

All of us approach any subject with a fair amount of bias. The same is true in politics and religion or spiritual stance. In my case, I stand in the place of the Christian life or in other words, I stand on the Word of God and His influence on my life and thoughts. Having said that, I will be putting forth my idea of the state of America and the problems that exist upon the writing of this book out of that place. There is an old church Hymn where the chorus goes something like this:

On Christ, the solid rock I stand,
All other ground is sinking sand.

I have heard that if you do not make a decision on something, you are basically making a decision. You have decided not to decide.

If there are no moral absolutes, then anything goes, there is no right or wrong. Abortion is okay, open borders are okay. Going to war is okay. Flying planes into tall buildings is okay.

There seems to be a whole new paradigm in our country that has permeated every nook and cranny of our society. In Psalms 90, the scripture tells us to number our days. So as American citizens, we need to make every day of our lives count to preserve the freedoms we enjoy.

I believe that everyone has a place, even if it's hidden well deep in their subconscious that they see and speak from. That is their foundation for living. That is their foundation for their belief system. That foundation may come from their parents, education or just their environment. The problem with that kind of foundation is that it can be influenced or shaken by the winds of time and by circumstances that they have to navigate through.

Let me be very clear as to where my foundation is coming from. In this country we have a supreme law of the land, that being the Constitution. Although there are men who would try to change what that document says, it does not move. For years, perhaps decades we have tended to put people above our constitution instead of having the supreme law, we have changed or interpreted it to suit the people or the populace of the country. The constitution is a living document. If we negotiate a compromise just to make a certain situation to make us comfortable that does not line up with the supreme law, the constitution, we reap the consequences.

I have realized lately that sometimes, when we are reading some article or book, that sometimes the smallest word in a sentence can make all the difference as to how our mind interprets the material. Let me give you an example. In scripture, John 14:6, John the apostle says about Christ, "I am THE way, THE truth and THE life." Had I not capitalized the word "the", our minds center on the words, "way, truth, life" which are important but not the most important. The word "THE" explains to us that there is no other way or no other truth, or no other life, except Christ. Maybe we need to use upper case "THE" when speaking of the, "THE Constitution"

After saying all that to say this. My foundation is in the Word of God, as recorded in our Holy Bible and in Jesus Christ, the foundation of my faith. Any thoughts and words in this book come from that vantage point and foundation.

Since the creation of man, we have broken laws. Since Adam and Eve ate of the forbidden fruit and disobeyed God we have decided that we know as much as God and do our own thing, making ourselves into Gods. WE thought we could put ourselves above God and His laws. The thing that is so concerning to me is the fact that we have come to the point that we believe that there is no absolute truth. Because of this, if there is no objective truth, there is no possibility for error. When there is no foundation, the building or society will fall. We have seen recently that it is beginning to happen, even with all of our advances in technology and communication and information we are really no better off.

It seems that in America the unthinkable has become tolerable. From there it becomes acceptable and then the acceptable becomes legal and many times the legal begins to be celebrated.

I have heard once that in order for evil to triumph, it only takes good people to say nothing.

If it appears that I am insinuating that the Church is to blame for the problems that we are having in our country and our government system. That possibly is partially true. What I am saying is that the moral temperature of our country must be laid at the feet of Christian people.

There are three areas that must be cultivated, if any faith is to be a living faith, the inner life of devotion, the intellectual life of thought and the outer life of human service. The weakness in the church, people's lives, is that there is no belief. If there is no sound belief, there is no action (service). If the church were to really believe in their faith, they would not allow the moral decay of our country. When was the last time you had a Jehovah Witness or Christian church at your door. I know for me, it has been quite a while since I have seen any kind of Evangelism going on.

The question today is not whether we know what's wrong with our country—we see that our government is infringing upon the rights of the people. Nor is the question whether we have ways of fixing it. Our founders have given us in the Constitution ways to fix it. The question is if we have the courage and knowledge to stand up to those who think that they have the power to do what they do without restraint.

Recently, in trying to help my adult son think through some difficulties that he was going through, I discovered that some of the "truths" that I have tried to base my life on are relative to other people. Does that mean there are no concrete truths in this world?

I believe there are concrete truths that we can rely on. Just like gravity is a concrete physical law, truth, there are moral, spiritual laws, truths, which remain true, no matter what anyone thinks about it. We can test those moral truths, just like we can test the law of gravity. When we jump off a ten-story building to test the truth of gravity, the result of when we hit the concrete below (pun intended). The same is true of moral laws. You can either decide to live by those moral laws or not. If not, then you will reap the consequences by hitting the proverbial concrete. Whether it's a physical law or moral law, you will not like the breaking of the law.

We have always had a cold civil war going on in the hearts of men to either bow to the absolute moral law of God or not. Our country and our world are just inches away from hitting the concrete. Is there time to put a safety net down before we hit? I am not sure, but we must try before our children hit the concrete.

In the Introduction of this book I will set forth the purpose of this book and the direction I intend to go with the ideas that I believe have gotten America to the place where we are today.

First, I believe this country has been founded on the principles based in God's word and the founders, while not ascribing to a national religion, but meant that these principles were of utmost importance for America to remain prosperous and a world leader in Freedom and economic success.

Again, having said that, I believe that the scriptures set down the establishing of four God ordained institutions and specific responsibilities to each of those three institutions.

At the beginning of our nation, the founders at the Constitutional Convention, made the Law i.e. the Constitution, but in these modern times, we have made the populace, people, the supreme thing, so the law changes at the whim of the populace.

Those four institutions being:

- The Family
- The Community
- The Church
- The Government

I probably should include in this treaty on the problems in our culture today, the fact that the family is made up of, first, the marriage covenant, and secondly, the offspring of that union. Our leaders, the Supreme Court specifically, has redefined not only the definition of marriage but even what gender means. We do not have offspring of two people but we have an educational system that raises our children.

Because the four institutions were created by God and defined by God and instituted by God, the enemy is attaching all these simultaneously, and as of 2019 we are losing this fight. All four are becoming re-defined and breaking down at the seams.

We must return these four God ordained institutions to their God defined original place and redefine them to their responsibilities that God intended them to be.

We have driven God out of our public squares, out of our government, out of our instruction of our children, out of our culture, and out of our lives. And by driving God out, we have created a vacuum. Into that vacuum our enemy has brought in still more gods. Our lives are now permeated with idols and increasingly carnal, materialistic and fragmented.

That which in earlier times would have shocked the nation's moral sensibilities no longer do so.

It appears to me that all four of the above institutions have been corrupted and are probably on the verge of destruction. As the scripture says in John 10:10, "The thief comes only to steal and kill and destroy". He has done that within all four institutions.

In each following chapters I will discuss the history of each institution, the problems that have contributed to the failure of each institution, the solutions to bring each institution back into compliance with their God-given responsibilities.

In our discussion of where, philosophically, we stand on a subject, it is imperative, that we be consistent in our belief system to arrive at the objective truth.

Case in point, as of the writing of this book, the government is in a deep debate about immigration and the closing of our southern border by building a wall across our borders. Several years ago, when we had a democratic president, the democratic side of congress was all for the wall and closing our borders. However now that we have a republican president, suddenly the democratic side of congress is vowing to bring all sorts of laws and power to keep the president from doing what earlier they were vowing to make happen. This brings destruction to both sides as far as integrity goes.

What we really desperately need today is the literature of witness in which men who have reached a firm place to stand are able to tell us the road by which they have come and why it was taken. We need a whole new group of thinkers who are willing and able to obey the injunction of I Peter 3:15-16, being prepared to make a defense of the "hope that is in them: but doing it "with gentleness and reverence." The result may be that the word apology will lose its present connotations.

SECTION I

The Family

CHAPTER 1

When we hear the word, "family", we all have some idea of what it means. Most of us live in what we would call a "family setting". In fact, families come in many different forms, and coming up with a single definition of the word is surprisingly difficult. In a legal sense, the word describes many relationships; for example, between parents and children, among people related by blood, marriage or adoption; or among any group of people living together in a single household.

Because the word "family" does not have a single meaning, laws often specify a definition. A zoning law, which seeks to set aside certain areas for single-family homes, may define family one way. Laws regulating insurance or government benefits may define it in some other way. Sociologist have their own definition, a family is a group of people related by marriage, blood, or adoption.

While the concept of family may seem simple and familiar to us, the family is a complex social unit with many facets, and no other social institution has a greater impact on the life and behavior of the individual.

Sociologist make a further distinction about family. A person's family of orientation is the one into which a person is born. It provides a person with his or her name, an identity and a heritage. It gives the person an ascribed status in the community. A, place to belong. The family of orientation "orients" children to their community and society and locates them in their world.

Perhaps, since our divorce rate is going through the roof, and there are so many broken homes, it is no wonder that we have several generations that have lost their way. They have no center to draw their identity from. They have received no orientation to their world.

The nuclear family, the smallest grouping of individuals that can be called a family is made up of a parent or parents and any children. The extended family consists of two or more adult generations of the same family whose members share economic resources and live in the same household. Extended family may also contain close relatives, such as grandparents, grandchildren, aunts, uncles and cousins.

HOW FAMILY STRUCTURES DEVELOPED

The development of agriculture and industry shaped society. These developments also shaped the family structure.

In the first human societies, family activity revolved around the hunting and gathering of food. Small bands of nuclear families followed herds of animals during the changing seasons, moving constantly.

Eventually, human beings developed the capacity to cultivate crops and domesticate animals. With the ability to grow food in a single location came a change in family structure. Families began to settle down in a single place. Family life focused on farming which required large numbers of workers, parents then tended to have more children. Extended families grew, and division of labor began to appear, with different family members performing different specialized tasks.

As technology developed and societies eventually moved from agricultural economies to industrialization, the extended family was slowly replaced by the nuclear family. Industrial life did not require large families for agricultural work. In fact, industrial economies tended to favor smaller family units with fewer mouths to feed and greater mobility. Postindustrial economies, such as our own, favor similar types of families.

I believe that the postindustrial society has contributed to the destruction of our family unit because of all the pressures living in this society and the lack of bonding in the family unit.

Perhaps this is the cause of a great many divorces, the pressure to legalize abortion and the increasing of the suicide rate.

I suppose that I should have started out with the individual as it takes at least two individuals to make up a family. It also takes two people to make up a relationship. When we talk about a family, we must talk about relationships. When you mix two individuals together, you begin a relationship that could go a myriad different directions.

As we all know, in our country, the divorce rate is skyrocketing. Every year we find many of our school age children living in a one parent family, for various and obvious reasons. The family unit is being attacked from all sides. From divorce to the accepting of same sex marriages which if left unchecked will make a trend to end humans. (I Corinthians). When Satan started out to destroy the world and the society that inhabits this world, his method was to first, destroy the family and thus destroying society. We no longer have strong families and thus the foundation of society.

I noticed recently, an ad on TV, where a young boy was spending time with his Dad playing on the Dad's internet Wi-Fi, which was supposedly really fast. Then the Ad cuts to the mom picking the boy up and he makes a comment about how fast Dad's internet is. The mom hands the boy a box of cookies and says, "Mom's cookies are pretty special too." Probably a pretty accurate picture of our society today including the divorced Mom and Dad competing for a child's affection.

From creation of Adam to the creation of Eve to begin the first family unit and the struggles of two human beings trying to relate, emotionally, mentally, and physically. The family unit has always been the foundation of the human race and society in general. The biological family unit became the societal unit, and finally a community unit. I will begin our discussion with, of course, the creation of the world and the human race, beginning with Adam and then Eve.

In the beginning, man and woman lived in paradise with everything they needed to survive at their disposal. God had supplied all their physical, emotional and spiritual needs there in the garden, where they were in perfect union with the environment and their creator. God told Adam that all "this" is yours to be used and enjoyed except for the fruit of the tree in the center of the garden. If they ate this fruit they would have the knowledge of "good" and "evil". If you are any kind of student of the Bible, you know the rest of the story. The serpent deceived Eve and she ate of the fruit and proceeded to give Adam the same fruit and they were no longer in perfect union with God or the environment. Two things are interesting to me in this scenario. First, where was Adam when Eve was deceived, because Adam was to be the overseer of everything, including Eve. He was to be the protector of Eve and he failed to be there to ward off the serpent and prevent the separation of a union with the woman and his creator. Why was Adam not asking questions of Eve, as she gave him the fruit to eat? "Where did you get this fruit? Why did you take it from the tree in the center of the garden, when God, our Father said not to eat of that fruit?" Those questions come quickly to my mind, as well as others.

Second, I always wonder what would have happened to the human race if instead of trying to hide the disobedience of God's command, and instead went to God and confessed their sin and asked for forgiveness. Adam and Eve hid from God as He came to meet with them. Of course, they could not actually hide from God as he is all knowing but they tried to hide from Him as they knew they were naked, as in their sin, was showing and they could not allow God to know who they really were. Sound familiar? As human beings we continue to hide our brokenness and disunity. We hide from one another. We hide from our families and spouses. We don't allow anyone too close, so they find out how ugly and broken we really are. Perhaps this is the actual sin, or at least the result of the sinfulness of humankind. What we need to realize is that we are all broken, and with sin, and are not perfect. One of the things that the original sin brought into our lives is that we have turned inward and brought the attention to ourselves. Before the fall, I think that Adam and Eve had the idea of pleasing God and had not thought of pleasing themselves. Then as they ate the forbidden fruit, their vision became turned to pleasing themselves. Thus, the marriage relationship became "How can I get my needs met?" instead of "How can I please God by serving my partner?"

It doesn't take much research to see how the family came to be established. Let's look at some of the references in biblical history to the family and the responsibilities that God ordained.

I suppose the major purpose for the family is to procreate and multiply to cover the earth with human kind. But even a greater purpose is to develop children to become God-- fearing and God--worshipping adults, who will also procreate and develop their children to do the same thing and on and on and on.

I have heard and have preached numerous sermons on Adam and Eve's sin of disobedience. This is probably the basis for all sin. Disobedience. James 4:17 says,

> "If anyone, then, knows the good they ought to do and doesn't do it, it is sin for them"

We find the answer to the purpose of the family in the following scripture text, that of teaching children to be obedient to the Word of God.

> And now, Israel, listen carefully to these decrees and regulations that I am about to teach you. Obey them so that you may live, so you may enter and occupy the land that the Lord, the God of your ancestors, is giving you. Do not add to or subtract from these commands I am giving you. Just obey the commands of the Lord your God that I am giving you....
>
> Look, I now teach you these decrees and regulations just as the Lord my God commanded me, so that you may obey them in the land you are about to enter and occupy. Obey them completely, and you will display your wisdom and intelligence among the surrounding nations.
>
> But watch out! Be careful never to forget what you yourself have seen. Do not let these memories escape from your mind as long as you live! And be sure to pass them on to your CHILDREN AND GRANDCHILDREN. Never forget the day when you stood before the Lord your God at Mount Sinai, where he told me, "Summon the people before me, and I will personally instruct them. Then they will learn to fear me, as long as they live. And they will teach their CHILDREN to fear me also. (NLT)

Deuteronomy 4:1--2; 5--6; 9--10

Also in Deuteronomy 29:18 God has given us these instructions that concern the family.

"I am making this covenant with you so that no one among you—no man, woman, clan, or tribe—will turn away from the Lord our God who worship these gods of other nations and so that no root among you bears bitter and poisonous fruit"

God has also given us a warning that if we do not keep following Him and His word we will reap the consequences:

Pour out your wrath on the nations that refuse to acknowledge you—on the people that do not call upon your name. For they have devoured your people Israel; they have devoured and consumed them, making the land a desolate wilderness." (Jeremiah 10:25)

Someone once said, "You can teach what you know, but you only reproduce who you are". We can teach to our children what we know through our own experience and what has been taught to us, but to reproduce in our children, how we want them to live, we must live out our value system.

As I am writing this, I have just come through a very difficult time in our family. Within a few days, three days, I have lost first my sister from a long battle with cancer, and two days later my older brother from a long battle from a stroke and other complications. The loss of my only two siblings has brought a very struggle with my purpose of living for however long the Lord sees fit to leave me on this earth. I believe that this book and the figuring out how I can help turn this country around is the reason that I am still here.

I think that the reason that our country is in the condition that it finds itself in is simply because of the enemy's destruction of the family unit. As we unite in family units, and thus become a nation made up of strong family units, we will see our country begin to turn a corner and get back on track. If, and only if, the family unit will be based on the teachings God has given us in His word.

The family unit is the stronghold of a nation. Once you have destroyed the family unit, you will begin to dismantle and destroy a nation and community.

When the Israelites left Jerusalem and went into captivity in Egypt, their country had been destroyed. So they returned to Jerusalem and their city and country laid in ruins. Nehemiah brought the people together to rebuild the wall (protection) around Jerusalem. He called each family to stand in the gaps and begin to rebuild the wall and in time, the whole city. Nehemiah knew that the family unit was the key to bringing the nation back from destruction.

One of the main things that has been a factor in the destruction of the family is the sin of Pride. We think that we have a corner on knowledge and wisdom, and we do not need God, His word, or His direction. That began way back in the Garden of Eden when we did not follow His word and disobeyed and became wise in our own eyes.

As this nation began, the wilderness, which was here as they landed on these shores presented a huge challenge to the settlers. The only way that they could survive was to help each other. One family helping another family building the physical house or barn or helping when a crisis struck the community. In our modern society, we have the mindset that we don't need each other. We can get through things and build our own little world. Even more than that, we make government our God and rely heavily on the government to take care of us.

The enemy knows that the way to destroy civilization and a nation is to destroy the foundation. It is not the physical infrastructure of a nation that is the foundation of a nation or civilization but relationships between its inhabitants. First, the destruction of the relationship between two people, a man and a wife, and then the family unit is separated and destroyed. The chink in the chain has been destroyed and removed and thus the nation and civilization are weakened and eventually continues to erode and, in the end, destroyed.

I ran across the following saying, in one of my classes:

Watch your thoughts,
They become words.
Watch your words,
They become actions.

Watch your actions,
They become habits.
Watch your habits,
They become your character
Watch your character
It becomes your destiny.

It has occurred to me that we cannot stop this process but only watch the consequences. All thoughts and actions have consequences, rather good or bad consequences. Those consequences will either be to our detriment or betterment. Everything that has ever been created, developed, invented has started out as a thought. On the flip side of that, anything that has been destroyed, collapsed, or became obsolete, started as a thought. Either as a thought of destroying or a new thought of something better. I remember my father always said, "If it was possible in the mind of man, it is possible."

The small laptop computer on which I am typing these words, started out as an idea in someone's mind. I know very little about computers, but I know that they are based on mathematical system in an intricate system that comes out on the screen with these words. Even the math started out in someone's mind. Everything starts in the mind. Solomon states in Proverbs, "As a man thinks, so is he"

In Isaiah 55:8, the prophet shares the message of God,

> "My thoughts are nothing like your thoughts" says the Lord. "And my ways are far beyond anything you could imagine. For just as the heavens are higher than the earth, so my ways are higher than your ways and my thoughts higher than your thoughts."

The problem that arose when Adam and Eve disobeyed God and took the fruit, is their thoughts became at war with God's. We decided that because we became wise in our own eyes, that we knew better how to act and think about our lives and relationships. All through the New Testament, the recurring theme is that Christ came to impart to us His power to *"be ye transformed by the renewing of the mind" (Romans 12:1).*

I am continually amazed at how connected our hearts (spiritually) are to our minds. Many counselors advise people to change their self-talk, i.e. their thoughts, their thinking to think better of themselves.

This thought life has affected the foundation of the family. Marriages break apart because the thought life becomes very selfish and self-centered, instead of the loving thought process that is projected towards our mates. Because the children see this thought process lived out in the parents, they become selfish and aware of their needs being met and when the next generation of parents get together, the process continues, and on and on, generation after generation.

I am convinced that the main reason our marriages are being destroyed on a daily basis is selfishness. We all come into a relationship with expectations and when those expectations are not met then we will find something or someone to fulfill those expectations. The other side of that coin is the lack of commitment to the things that matter. Our society is built on getting what we want, in an instant. When our wants do not get met in the next moment then we jump ship and go to the next thing. We need, in our relationships to be selfless and commit to our relationships with God first, then people.

I am the product of a broken home. My parents were divorced when I was a sophomore in College. I can remember crying myself to sleep in my dorm room after hearing that my parents were splitting up. No more "home" to go home to. No safe place to return to. I needed to become an individual, instead of part of a family unit. It was not a happy time in my life.

Fifty years later, I find myself in the somewhat the same place. After 25 years of marriage, my wife and I divorced. I will not go into the details of the broken marriage but suffice it to say that I had not "renewed my mind". I remarried a wonderful woman that I believe God lead me to and we have been together for 23 years and counting.

Recently, my, 45-year-old, son experienced going through a divorce and it has been even more excruciating than when I went through it. And the battle keeps raging with the enemy of our thought life.

In many foreign cultures, the family is one of the most important parts of the culture. The family is so important in these cultures that if one of the family members, embarrasses the family, they are disowned and can never again call themselves a part of the family. Fortunately, in America, that is not the case. Another part of that foreign culture is that the family is a larger unit than just the immediate family. Grandparents, and even great grandparents are a part of that unit. The younger members are expected to care for the older members, to the extent of housing and feeding, and taking care of their medical needs.

The culture in the New Testament, was much the same. I think of the parable of "the prodigal son". He was a member of a larger family unit. He wanted to strike out on his own and take what he thought was his part of the family inheritance. The difference in this parable is that the father never disowned his son but let him go and when he returned, welcomed him with open arms and love.

We have lost, in America, the importance of the family unit. We have lost the determination to teach and instruct family members the truth about how the world is supposed to work in God's plan. I would like to discuss in the following pages where and when we have lost the importance of the family in our culture in the United States of America.

God established the institution of marriage before the church, before civil societies, and before government. From this God initiated relationship of marriage, all life is formed, birthed, and given priceless oversight. We do not replace what God supernaturally created and established with anything proposed by any person, people, government, or court. Family is the first vital cell of society. It is the foundation of government. Government did not create marriage. God did.

In 2015, the US Supreme Court redefined marriage, paving the way for a flood of detrimental policies and practices. Families are being destabilized, children are being raised in psychologically damaging environments, and religious freedom is being threatened. This is very serious."

Since true marriage only works between a man and a woman, no one has any more right to gay marriage than he or she has the right to sprout wings and fly. Government does not grant rights. It only recognizes rights given to us by our creator.

Often as I have studied and lead several churches through the process of developing a mission statement, trying to define what we are to be doing as a group of called out believers that it is imperative to keep that statement and ideas in front of the congregation many times over the course of years or even decades. We as human beings and even Christians tend to forget that which we do not see consistently in front of us. The same is true, that which our founding fathers brought together in the Declaration of Independence and Constitution of our great country will soon be forgotten if our schools and leaders do not consistently keep in front of us.

CHAPTER 2

Early America

Our current president, Donald Trump, has said that he wants to, "Make America Great Again". I think that to do this, we must bring back the family culture to America. The family should be the most important thing in our culture. The enemy of this world, Satan, has come to destroy what is good, which includes the family unit. The current rate of divorce in our country is edging toward 70%. Many children in our schools come from broken homes. Which means that they are coming into our classrooms with emotional, and psychological problems before they can even start to learn. Not only is the enemy destroying the family but also the educational process.

When God established the family unit and gave the family the responsibility to raise, nurture and educate children, so that the human race could multiply and succeed, He made the family unit the most important unit in the world. If the family unit is the most important unit in the world, the best thing the enemy can do is to disrupt and destroy the foundation of civilization, which is the family. The divorce rate and the increasing empowering of LPGT community is destroying the family unit in our culture and many other cultures.

In early America, laws were enacted to make sure that the family unit was strong and stayed together. There was a time in New England that it was considered so important for people to be in families, that the legal system took steps to ensure that everyone was. The provinces of Connecticut and Plymouth passed laws that made it illegal for a single person to live alone. These were not idle laws. The records indicate that in

1668, in Middlesex County, Massachusetts, the court searched the town for single people and placed them in families (Thomas Anderson).

Order in the family was of paramount importance to the Puritans. In Massachusetts, the selectmen and constables of each town were required to periodically inspect families to make sure they maintained "good order". If the family fell into disorder, they were to remove the children and put them in families where there was order.

The Quakers of Pennsylvania believed that the primary role of the family was to raise its children and to promote the spiritual health of its members. This biblical view made family one of the most important things in all creation. In God's eyes, a family is the cure for loneliness.

God sets the solitary in families. Psalms 68:6

Now, I need to make clear that I do not believe that you can legislate morality. Morality comes from within, some of which can be taught and caught by example.

I think that one of the reasons that the family is so important is that when we are alone, it can be dangerous in our own lives. We used to hear a lot the saying, "An idle mind is the devils workshop." When we are alone, Satan can come and make our minds do funny things. In the last few years, we have had many mass shootings in schools, malls etc. Many of those perpetrators have been people who have been bullied and feel alone. In that loneliness the mind begins to go to dark places, if those people had been in good, strong families, perhaps they would have had a safe place to go and talk and be cared for.

We cannot assume that the struggles of the family unit is a modern day event. There have always been struggles in the family from rebellious children, to parents making poor decisions. In the years leading up to the revolutionary war statistics tell us that a lot of children were conceived before marriage. Parents would sometimes take drastic measures to hide the shame of a daughter who was pregnant before marriage. Of course the parents were forced to give permission to marry many times to avoid the shame.

Family was everything back in our early days as a country.

A single person had little stability and really no place in the community. There has never been a time in the history of America that the family was not important. Probably more so now than ever before.

In my studies of early American history, it is interesting to note that when the English set up companies to settle the new world, they set them up as colonies that would function as a unit. In other words, a commune. Each individual and family would be responsible to do some of the work and share in the products that were harvested. After a period of time, some of the people, decided they would not have to work as hard and still could partake of the harvest. Of course, production went down and for a couple of winters, consequentially the colonist did not have enough to eat. Some starved to death. Some wanted to return to England. After several tries to plant a settlement in the new world using this method, they returned to the concept of the family being the central unit and the family would work for themselves and this was proven to be a successful endeavor. No matter how many communes anybody invents, the family always creeps back. Almost all of history proves that the family unit is indispensable.

In the early days of our country, as the settlers, settled into towns, they were usually around an agriculture center. You didn't live very close to your neighbors, geographically. But as people would go through hardships or crises, neighbors were right there to help. Harvesting crops, caring for the sick, etc. I look around now as people have gathered into cities because of the industrial changes that have happened over the years, I see six-foot fences around homes. Automatic garage door openers so we don't have to get out of our cars and in most cases even see or know our neighbors at any level. We have fortresses that our neighbors cannot break through. Not only have our families been splintered, but our communities have been splintered. As I am writing this book, there is a great concern about security especially electronic social media. We have hundreds of friends on Facebook or twitter and yet we "know" no one person at all.

I have walked into restaurants and observed a family of four or five sitting waiting for their meal to be served or even eating and every one of them on their mobile devices. I am assuming that this is what their home life is like also. By the way, when are we going to stop calling those things, "phones"?

Many societies have tried to make the state more important than the family unit. The efforts, for the most part, have been unsuccessful. Germany and Hitler are the first to come to mind. Their education system was set up to indoctrinate children to draw their allegiance away from their parents and to the state as being supreme. I am afraid that the education system in America is almost at that point. As the family unit has been ordained by God and given the responsibility of nurturing and educating children. The key problem in the family right now is that, most families have abdicated that responsibility to the state, the government. Education is not the responsibility of the state. Never has been and never will be.

Someone once put it, "Marriage is the greatest 'anti-poverty' program God ever created

Both parents don't necessarily have to hold down a job, one paycheck from a gainfully employed Dad with mom at home taking care of the kids, is better than a single mother living off welfare."

I will say more about welfare in the next section on the "Church"

Back in the late 60's, 7 percent of kids were born out of wedlock. Today, 40 percent of all kids in America are to unwed mothers. Government is now the father to far too many homes.

In most societies around the world there is a ceremony or rite that ushers' young boys into manhood and the responsibilities of manhood. In America there is no point at which boys become men. In ancient Egypt there were kings who took on that title at ages 12 or younger. Much of the problem in America is because we have too many absent fathers to train them into manhood.

In America, 29% of white children are born to a single mother but 72% of black children are born out of wedlock. Children born out of wedlock are exponentially more likely to abuse drugs, drop out of school, commit crimes, and be incarcerated*

"The Father Factor", National Fatherhood Initiative, http: www.Fatherhood.org/mdedia,consequences-of-father-absence-statistics.

Many times throughout scripture, God is referred to as Father, as in the Lord's Prayer: "Our Father who art in Heaven…" We have sung in church the song, "You're a good, good Father." Of course, the writer is using a metaphor in calling God, Father. No metaphor is perfect. But

God is not an "it". He is a person who we can have a relationship with. The writers in scripture, when using the term Father when referring to God, are using it to give a better idea of who God is. The problem is that earthly fathers, even though we love our children, are not perfect. We make mistakes. WE don't show our love in a perfect way. Our resources fall way short to take care of our children. That does not take away our love for our children. WE know that no matter what our children do or say does not diminish the love we have for them. In that sense, we can call God, "Our Father"

Because of the absence of so many fathers in our family units in our country the family is absent of their leader and example of an all caring God.

FAMILY WITHOUT GOD IS JUST PROCREATION!!

CHAPTER 3

Educational Responsibility

"The aim of Education is the knowledge, not of facts, but of values"
Williams Burroughs

"So, commit yourselves wholeheartedly to these words of mine. Tie them to your hands and wear them on your forehead as reminders. Teach them to your children. Talk about them when you are at home and when you are on the road, when you are going to bed and when you are getting up. Write them on the doorposts of your house and on your gates, so that as long as the sky remains above the earth, you and your children may flourish in the land the Lord swore to give your ancestors"

Deuteronomy 11: 18--21

In one of the churches that I was privileged to pastor in the state of Washington, we sponsored a private Christian School. Whenever a parent would apply to put their child in the school, we were careful to tell them that they were responsible to educate their child and we were only there to assist them. The school had a student body of about 80 students, grades K-12. We operated on the basis that it was biblically ordained that parents had the responsibility to educate their child with a Christian foundation.

The parents were also made aware that we had a corporal punishment policy and that if we deemed it necessary to invoke that punishment that they would administer the punishment in our presence. I might also add, that our church was located in a logging, fishing community on the coast. We only had to call a parent out of the forest or off a boat once to punish a child. They made sure it did not happen again.

I once heard a speaker at a convention, who happened to be a Doctorate in Education say the, "worst thing to happen in public education was mandatory education laws". I am sure he was referring to the fact that students had to be there even if the desire to learn was not there. Somehow, we must, as parents, not extinguish the desire to learn in our children.

One of the most interesting things about our society, I think, is the fact that we want our children to not grow up to fast. We have come up with terms to use to describe our children, so they don't grow to be adults to fast. Terms such as "teenagers" or "adolescence" or "youth". Where did we come up with these terms?

We see, in our study of history, that ancient societies that children went from being children to adults. It usually happened around the age of 12. Many societies had rituals that were thrust upon children that brought them into adulthood. Even the Jewish religion has a ritual to bring children into adulthood. "Bar mitzvah" Some tribes in Africa, take their children who have become of age, into the wilderness and they must survive on their own. When they pass this test, they go through a ceremony where they celebrate becoming a man, or adult.

So, I conclude from that the most appropriate style of education would be home schooling. Since when do we let beauracrats tell us who is qualified to teach our children?

During my tenure as pastor of a church, we decided to open a Christian School in our building. Since my wife happened to be a state certified teacher, she over saw the educational portion of the school. During the growth of the school we hired probably 4-5 teachers; some certified and some not.

Whenever I had parents come to our school to wish to enroll their child, I would always sit down and discuss the school and our mission. I always stated that our mission was to assist parents in their God ordained responsibility to educate their child. That we were not a place where parents could drop their child off and expect them to come out educated.

At the end of our conversations, I would ask if they had any questions that I might answer. There were always two questions that were asked by every parent. (1) Is your school state approved?

My answer to that was always, "Is the school where your child is now state approved". They were usually coming from public school so the answer was always, "yes". Most parents had little knowledge of what that process was all about. It actually had little to do with the educational process, but the safety of the students and building codes.

The second question proved to be the most interesting. (2) Are your teachers state certified? I would always answer that question with a question: "Are the teachers where your child is now, state certified?" More times than not, they were coming from the public schools, so their answer was always "yes". I would continue the conversation with, "If those are your two criteria, and the school that your child is in now, meet that criteria, then why you wish to have your child come here? Most of the time they wished to have their child get a good education and be more than just a number. And they would always bring up that their child's teacher could not teach. I responded to that by saying, the state said that they were qualified to teach. Is that not enough? I would always ask the parents if either one of them had ever had a teacher in their past that they knew could not teach. They would usually bring them up by name. Again, the state had said that they were qualified to teach. I will get into why this happens later in the next chapter.

Most people do not realize what being accredited even means. It simply means a higher entity accredits a lower entity by meeting certain criteria. Many people do not realize that the three top universities in our country started out by not being accredited by any association. Their reasoning was that there was no one higher than those schools to accredit them. Those schools being, Harvard, Yale and Princeton.

The National Educators Association or NEA have become one of our country's largest and strongest Union. They sometimes claim to not be a union, but they are as 90% of teachers belong to the organization. They fight the administrations across the country for higher pay and tenure for teachers. Our state governments will take on the task of certifying the teachers' credentials, accordingly to have a standard that teachers must meet. Because they have fought for tenure for teachers, the problems come when an administrator wants to weed out poor teachers and the teachers have fought for tenure, it becomes almost impossible to get rid of the poor teachers as the "law" is "last in, first out." So, you have a first or second year teacher that is a great teacher, but a longer tenured inept teacher remains, and the great teacher is let go. What has always confused me is that the state has already certified both teachers that they are acceptable. So, the problem is not with the teachers or the administration but the way we (government agencies) decide if someone has the aptitude to teach.

The mood in America today is that the government can and will fix the problems in front of the American people. The problem with the Educational systems we have in place is really all the fault of the family abdicating their responsibility of education to the government instead of resolving to take the God-given responsibility themselves.

President Ronald Reagan tried to abolish the Federal department of Education but did not succeed but instead the department got even bigger.

Dennis Prager, suggested in an opted he wrote for *National Review* in January 2017 says, "The Left so far is winning the war by injecting its views into students. Children in school, he says, learn that "virtually every war America fought was imperialist and immoral." That the free market is actually a system of oppression, that all the troubles that affect African Americans are the fault of racist white people, and that the "nuclear-family ideal is inherently misogynistic and homophobic."

> "That is how it has been able to take over our schools—from elementary schools to high schools to the universities— and indoctrinate America's young people; how it has taken over nearly all the news media; and how it has taken over the entertainment media" Prager also wrote.[1]

Some leaders in the public school system, when speaking about private or home schools say, "Parents are not smart enough to make decisions about their children's education." When I hear those comments, I think of several things. One is something I heard once that when someone points their finger at you, they have three pointing back at themselves. The second is something a counselor once said to me when I shared about someone who did not respect me in who I am or what I do and spoke bad about me. She responded by saying that it says more about them and who they are than about you.

Both of those statements describe about those public school administrators who say that parents are not smart enough to make decisions about their child's education. As I see it, most of those parents are products of the same education system that they are saying could do a better job of educating their child. To say that a product that you produced in your system is not smart enough, kind of, defeats the argument of your system.

These educators only argue against home schools and private schools to save their jobs. Studies have shown that private schools have a higher percentage of graduates and those who are accepted into the top universities in our country.

Also, public schools use private business's as venders to provide services that they cannot do as well, such as, food services, book publishers, Bus services and personnel services to provide support staff.

The goal to use the public-school system as a way to indoctrinate our children has existed for a long time. Back in the 1800's men like Robert Owen and Horace Mann saw the public schools as means to do just that. Mann believed that children belong to the state and should therefore be educated by the state. Among others, these men formed a secret society that pushed for public education. Orestes A. Brownson (1803-1876), a leader of this society, said, "The great object was to get rid of Christianity and to convert our churches into halls of science. The plan was not to make open attacks on religion...but to establish a system of state schools...from which religion was to be excluded, on which nothing was to be taught but such knowledge as is verifiable by the senses, and to which all parents were to be compelled by law to send their children..."

Later in 1930, C.F. Potter wrote "Humanism, A New Religion," in which he said, "Education is thus a most powerful ally of humanism and every American public school is a school of humanism. What can theistic Sunday schools, meeting for an hour once a week, and teaching only a fraction of the children, do to stem the tide of a five-day program of humanistic teaching"[2]

Fifty-three years later, in 1983, John Dunphy wrote an award-winning essay. He wrote,

I am convinced that the battle for human-kind's future must be waged and won in the public school classroom by teachers who correctly perceive their role as proselytizers of a new faith…these teachers must embody the same selfless dedication as the most rabid fundamentalist preachers, for they will be ministers of another sort, utilizing the classroom instead of a pulpit to convey humanist values in whatever subject they teach…The classroom must and will become an arena of conflict between the old and the new, the rotting corpse of Christianity, together with all its adjacent evils and misery and the new faith of humanism, resplendent in its promise of a world in which the never-realized Christian ideal of 'love thy neighbor' will finally be achieved.

What a diabolical masterplan! Establish schools where children are compelled by law to attend, often from the age of 4 in preschool all the way until they become legal adults and able to leave parental care. Let the schools be government-funded, of course. After all, if parents would pay for their children's education they'd feel entitled to have a say regarding what their children are learning and what activities they participate in. Fight hard to remove as much parental involvement as possible; recently going as far as not allowing the parent to know what classes/activities their child is participating in and denying the parent's right to remove their child from said activities. Instead, place counselors in schools that will be there for any child needing advice regarding their sexual orientation or an unwanted pregnancy or even showing respect for our country and the flag that represent our country. Forcefully remove the children's freedom to pray or read the Bible during their time in school. Meanwhile, indoctrinate them to disclaim such "outdated" notions as a Creator and absolute truth. As an alternative, drill the Humanist Manifesto into their impressionable minds.

So, the Humanist seem to be winning the battle, if not the war. How can we as concerned citizens, parents combat this system of control and indoctrination? That is a question I hope to give several solutions in the last section of this book.

As I am writing this, our country, actually the hold world is dealing with a pandemic of coronavirus (Corvid-19). This has basically shut the hold world down. We are practicing social distancing and trying to practice good hygiene by washing hands and using hand sanitizer. Most of the stores are closed and of course the schools are closed. Everyone is supposed to be sheltering at home, I was amazed when I saw a teacher post, I hope tongue in cheek, "We need to get students back in school before they start thinking for themselves."

Most, if not all of the schools have gone to online classrooms. They will do this for the remaining of the school year. I have several observations with this format. I think we can reduce cost for education by about half. No need to build large buildings that sit empty three months out the year. No need to heat them or air condition them. No need to pay someone to clean them. I might be possible to get along with building auditoriums and/or Gyms where music and drama and sports may occur. The other side of this coin is that parents can be more involved with their child's education. Tutors can be made available where needed. Online testing can occur. Students would be able to cover twice the materials in the same amount of time because of less distraction.

Someone once said that He who controls the past, controls the future. Thus, bringing to mind the actions of many today of taking down statues of our leaders who the powers that be do not agree with. The civil war and the confederates in the south are part of our history.

Another thing I have noticed while teaching in the public schools is that most of the time there is only a classroom set of textbooks. I have been told that this is because of budget constraints. Because there is just a classroom set of textbooks, the students are not able to take books home to do their homework. I am convinced that the budget constraints are not the primary reason behind this lack of materials. Unless the parents request to see any textbooks or curriculum, the parents have no idea what their child is learning or being influenced with or indoctrinated with. So, the progressive view point is free to influence many generations of people.

I am a firm believer in the voucher system in financing schools, rather public or private. That kind of funding allows parents to make those kinds of decisions for their children, rather than allow the government to say where and how their child is educated. The schools that produce a superior product (education) will stay in business. The poorer schools will be forced to close.

Spending levels on Kindergarten to twelfth-grade here in American public education is even more striking when compared with those of other developed "first world" nations on the international stage. According to the Organization for Economic Cooperation and Development (OECD), only Luxembourg and Norway spend more per child than the United States, and Luxembourg's spending is skewed because of its status as an international financial center with a very small national population. All other countries the OECD surveyed spend dramatically less than the United States.

Despite the enormous and unparalleled costs, America's public schools are performing poorly, and many are failing. The Program for International Student Assessment (PISA) is an international organization affiliated with the OECD that periodically administers standardized proficiency test to fourth graders and fifteen-year-olds in schools in sixty-five countries. These results are analyzed and made available to participating countries for near- and long-term education budgeting and planning. The PISA 2012 results were published a few years ago and they point to a failing American educational system. If you were in the market to buy a house and most of the houses failed to meet code or building standards, you would not buy a house that any of those builders built. Why, then, would you send your children to a failed system?

One of the things that give private schools more leverage to provide a better education is the fact that the good private schools usually have waiting list to get in to their school. If a student does not behave and perform at a certain level, he is out the door and someone who wants to be there will take their place. With a voucher system, all schools will have that same leverage.

As a personal example of this indoctrination of our education systems, let me share an experience that I had a few months ago. As I have previously stated, I do some substitute teaching in our cities public school system. On one particular day, as they do every day, stand and do the pledge of Allegiance to the flag. I noticed about half the class did not stand. When the pledge was over, and the announcements were given over the intercom, I proceeded to give a lecture about giving the flag due respect by standing. When classes were over, I went to the office and asked them, what the district policy is towards standing for the pledge. I was told that all students have a choice, whether to stand or not. Again, the liberal influence on our education system.

I learned recently that one of the goals of the Muslim religion is to gain control of our public-school system in order to indoctrinate children into the Islamic faith. Never underestimate the power of education. When the door is shut, the teacher lives in his or her own world with an immense amount of power over young minds.

On one occasion, while substituting, I was glancing through a history book. I noticed that there was a page and a half on the Islam religion and a couple of paragraphs on Christianity. It seems a bit skewed towards another thought pattern than what this country was founded upon.

I learned several years ago that there was a teacher in one of the public schools that was honored to be teacher of the year at that school. She was a first year teacher. Because of budget cuts, she was not hired for the next year because the teachers union says that last in are first to go. So a teacher that maybe not a good teacher was rehired, while a great teacher was let go. Unions do not belong in education because you cannot standardize their work. Lawyers and Doctors are not unionized because of the same reason. Maybe when we begin to realize this and use common sense, we will be on the road to success in education.

Common Core instructs teachers to present "informational texts"— such as Lincoln's Gettysburg Address—without any background information or context. So, while students will still read some important material they'll read it "cold", which will strip texts of their historical power and instead allow students to interpret the documents however they choose.

This kind of educational process leads students to believe that truth is as we interpret it, not as the facts bring to bear to the truth. I am thinking of the scripture that says, "As a man thinks, so is he" (Proverbs 23:7)

"The aim of education is the knowledge, not of facts, but of values." William S. Burroughs.

The government or the "state" has no business involved in the education process. It is not the government's God given responsibility to educate children. It is parents, family God given responsibility. I will discuss the governments God given responsibility in a later chapter. The government public school system is deathly against private or online education as they will lose control of how the next generation will be educated. Their main argument, as I have stated previously is that parents are not qualified to teach their own children. The question then arises, "By whose standards are we judging those parents" The government was never meant to be in control of the education of children,

David Gelernter, professor of computer science at Yale University, is looking ahead to how technology can be used to restore true parental control over the education process. To do that, he is proposing that Americans redefine the very idea of what constitutes a "public school". His concept is something he refers to as "local internet schools," and he recently explained how they might work:

> "The idea is simple: a one-classroom school, with twenty-odd children of all ages between 6th and 12th grade, each sitting at a computer and wearing mike-and-earphones. They all come from nearby. A one-room internet school might serve a few blocks in a suburb, or a single urban apartment house,

> In front sits any reliable adult whom the neighbors vouch for—often, no doubt some student's father (or mother), taking his turn. He leads the Pledge, announces regular short recesses to clear everyone's head, proclaim lunchtime. He hands out batteries and Ban-aids and sends sick children home or to a doctor. He reloads the printers and fusses with malfunctioning scanners, no doubt making any problem worse. But, these machines are cheap, and each classroom can deploy several.

> Each child does a whole curriculum's worth of learning online, at the computer. Most of the time he follows canned courses onscreen. But for an hour every day, he deals directly one to one over phone or videophone with a tutor. Ideally there's a teaching assistant on an open phone

line throughout the day, each assistant dealing with a few dozen students.

The online courses (some exist already, but not enough) are produced by teaching maestros. As these new schools gather momentum, they will make use, as tutors or assistants, of the huge number of people who are willing and able to help children in some topic for a few hours a week but can't or won't teach full time: college and graduate students, retirees, lawyers, accountants, housewives, professors.

Gelernter, also, added that parents would have to be committed [3]and on board with these and very much involved, such as taking their turn as supervisor or simply monitoring their child's progress.

When I read Mr. Gelernter's description of this "internet school", I thought back to the 80's when I administered a private Christian school. Our curriculum as self-paced and consisted of ten booklets per subject per grade level. Each student worked through the booklets at their own pace. Each subject was divided into hourly units guided by a teacher. We had what we called mastery learning. Students were tested on each booklet and had to score at least a 90% or higher before going on to the next booklet. Many of our students covered a year and a half work in one school year. We had 3-4 teachers for about 80 students grades K-12. We were giving students a great education for about half the cost that the public schools were doing and producing good results.

According to an article in "Bloomberg Businessweek of 3/25/19" by Ronesh Ratnesar entitled, "the way out of College Admissions hell is . . .video games."

It is not surprising that employers are not looking for people with more knowledge but people who can think and problem solve. The test that students take to be admitted to colleges, SAT and ACT are not really working.

Many have said this is the age of information or the age of education or knowledge. Statistics say that 1 in 3 Americans have at least a B.A. degree. However many of our businesses state that our colleges do not prepare students for the work force or business. They have learned wrote memory information but not how to solve problems. In other words, they have not been taught to think for themselves or to be creative and imaginatively. Studies have shown that high school teachers are teaching to take test but not how to think.

I have thought recently that our government is so corrupt that I am not sure that it can be righted. I think the same goes for our education system. Just recently a couple of rich Hollywood stars have been indicted for paying vast amounts of money so their child could get into the best colleges in the country. Some of them will serve jail time because of the corruption

There are people who are studying the topic of college admissions. Right now there are several million high school students who take the ACT test to gain entrance to colleges. Several more million will take the SAT test for admission. But still the businesses claim that the graduates are not ready for the business world as they cannot solve problems. Some researchers are experimenting with video games as a way of testing student's ability to solve problems and achieve a level of expertise to gain entrance to universities. If it proves to be more successful, we may see a change in the entrance exams to universities. It may take a while though, as we only have to follow the money trail to see where the power lies. The publishers of the tests and text books stand to lose lots of money, if the test prove to be inadequate to prepare for a higher education or readiness for the business world.

The question that needs answering is, "What do we teach." At the moment, in America, we are teaching what someone in an office somewhere has decided that this is what our children need to learn. The problem is that, those people are composing whatever theories and ideas are that they have decided on according to their philosophy. There is nothing wrong with any of that as far as the parents have a say in what their children are going to learn and what slant they want taught. However, our public education system only teaches from one direction. That being the direction that some committee has decided upon.

I am appalled at the lack of knowledge in the high school students on the subject of civics. We don't teach about the Constitution and how laws are written. We don't teach how our economic system works. If our young people were taught more about our government and how it works and how it has withstood time and wars for generations

If we were to privatize the education system, we could give the parents a diverse selection as to philosophy of teaching methods and what kind of standard they want taught to their children. I could see not only a diverse religious selection of schools but also academic levels. Especially at the secondary level. For instance, perhaps high schools for the arts, a high school for Math and Science, and perhaps one for the humanities. At each one the subject would be emphasized and gone more in depth. Perhaps even one for the trades, carpentry, mechanics.

I encourage all patriots, especially Christian patriots to pull your children out of public education. Place them in Christian schools or private schools that line up with your values. You may not be able to afford that kind of education for your children, so instead, home school. I am convinced that the left, progressives have taken over education in America. They are teaching our children leftist values and anti-American values. At the very least, check out text books that your children our being taught from. Get involved because you are responsible for your child's education. No one else.

EDUCATION THAT DOES NOT START
WITH GOD IS JUST MANIPULATION

SECTION II
The Community

CHAPTER 4

Once the family has been righted, then the community will be on its way to functioning properly.

Community bringing Order

I believe this is the area that the Church has failed the most. The Church is typically able to teach and impart standards for worship, morality and loving compassion that remind people of how they are to do life. The problem is these values tend to get locked up inside four walls of the buildings in which we gather, instead of influencing the communities in which we live.

Recently, during the Pandemic that effected the whole world, the church has had to take their worship to the internet and do video church into the homes of those who wish to participate. It has been an effective way to worship in the interim. However, it really has not made a lot of difference in getting the church outside of the walls of the church to affect the community.

In today's world, it seems that our communities are influencing the church rather than the church influencing the communities. Even our worship is becoming more and more Hollywood with the worship team performing with light shows and fog machines. The Christian sets in the audience and rarely participates in worship.

Jesus proclaims in Matthew 5:13 that we are to be the salt of the earth. If that were the case our world would look very different. The communities which are made up of families organizing for the "general welfare" these families living geographically close together would look very different.

Communities come together to govern themselves, that no family steps on another families rights or interferes with their daily patterns of life and their pursuit of happiness. Communities agree together for the rules, morals and values that will provide for life, liberty and the pursuit of happiness.

All community realities are realized and sustained through the family. The scripture says, "Our Father...for yours is the kingdom" (Matt. 6:9-13). Any time we leave the concept of family, we've left the subject of community. The family of God is God's target, and that family is community.

> "But you are not like that, for you are a chosen people. You are a royal priests, a holy nation. God's very own possession. As a result, you can show others the goodness of God, for he called you out of the darkness into his wonderful light.
>
> Once you had no identity as a people; now you are God's people. Once you received no mercy; now you have received God's mercy."
>
> II Peter 2:9--10

Salt in Jesus' illustration is about adding flavor to a community in the same way that is used to enhance the flavor of a meal. As of the writing of this book, I am on a low sodium diet because of a heart condition. Believe me, when I say that food has a different taste when it has salt added. I have been forced to eat very bland food because of my heart condition.

It makes a difference living your life with the salt of Jesus. Your life becomes an adventure and exciting. Without Jesus, your life is bland. Although it may seem like it has taste when it does not.

The church tends to think we are complete and the community needs us. While that is partly true, it's more true to say that we are able to be added to what already exist by God's design.

I recently heard a preacher say, "I have worked all my ministry to get the community inside these four walls, when I should have been getting people out of these walls into the community.

A lot of Christians join or become part of the church fellowship to escape the community, but maybe we need to look at it more about escaping the safety of the church to grab the supernatural that only God can do in the community.

There is an old African proverb that says, "If you want to go fast, go by yourself. If you want to go far, go together".

That is truth that bears out many times over. God has set humanity up in communities for a reason. As we try to establish God's Kingdom as it is in heaven here on earth, we must do it together. That is why God has established the church to be in community

As of this writing, America and the world is struggling with a pandemic with great consequences. Our economy is going down on a daily basis. The government has asked everyone to shelter in place. In other words, stay home. Which means that we are to practice social distancing, keeping away from one another in order to not spread the disease. Many people are struggling with depression and loneliness. Humans were created to be together. The scripture says that "it is not good for man to be alone". It is interesting that the old African proverb proves to be true. We want to eradicate the disease quickly so we are separated but for society to succeed in the long run, we must do it together.

CHAPTER 5

Serving One Another

Of course we can serve one another within the family unit and for the family to function properly, it must serve one another. However, we cannot express the giving spirit just within the family unit. It must extend to the community around us.

One of the greatest attributes of God that Christ himself, exemplifies is the attribute of giving or serving. The scripture says that Christ said the greatest in the kingdom will be the servant of all.

There are over 250 mentions of giving in the Bible. When the Corinthian church wanted to give an offering to the Macedonians, the Apostle Paul says this to them:

II Corinthians 9:12-15

"So, two good things will result from this ministry of giving—the needs of the believers in Jerusalem will be met, and they will joyfully express their thanks to God. As a result of your ministry, they will give glory to God. For your generosity to them and to all believers will prove that you are obedient to the Good News of Christ. And they will pray for you with deep affection because of the overflowing grace God has given to you. Thank God for this gift too wonderful for words."

When I go out to eat at a restaurant most of the time I am waited on by a waiter or waitress as the case might be. They will stand at my table and say something like, "Hi, my name is John, or Mary, I will be your server today. What can I get you to drink?" Right? Well, if they are expecting a tip in return for their serving, then they are not my servant but my employee. If they are not expecting anything in return other than the satisfaction of being helpful in doing something I either can't do for myself or do not wish to do for myself, then they become my server.

The definition of the word, servant, is "a personal or domestic attendant". It comes from the French word, "servant" meaning "foot soldier". The foot soldier serves at the wishes of the king or government leader. In other words we are to be foot soldiers in our communities and especially our homes. We teach our children to be servants by our example.

In order for us to do this, we must have our vision changed. My vision physically has been changed in more ways than one. I have been changed spiritually, or at least I hope it has. It has also been changed physically. About twenty years ago I had a detached Retina. After four surgeries to try and fix it so I could see again in that eye, I was rendered blind in that eye. Not to long after that, my wife and I went to a 3-D movie. After a few minutes into the movie, I leaned over to my wife and said, "It looks the same as it had the first time they released the movie" I was told later that in order to see 3D you must have two eyes. Because I did not have the use of both eyes, it was impossible for me to see 3D. The reason is that I have no depth perception. I have tried to keep my driving to a minimum because of this.

I say all that to say this. We must change our vision and start looking not at ourselves but at the needs of others. We have to see the elderly people next door that need things done that maybe we have never seen before. We need to see that single mom that needs child care or financial assistance. I have shared previously that we have six foot fences around our homes and garage door openers, so we can pull our cars into a garage and never have to see our neighbors. We have become a society that only looks out for ourselves, I am thinking that it was the same way when Christ walked the earth.

I am reminded of the story in John chapter five, about the paralytic waiting for someone to carry him into the pool when the water was disturbed to be healed.

One of the men lying there had been sick for thirty-eight years. When Jesus say him and knew he had been ill for a long time, he asked him, "Would you like to get well?"

"I can't, sir," the sick man said, "for I have no one to put me into the pool when the water bubbles up. Someone else always gets there ahead of me."

Jesus told him, "Stand up, pick up your mat, and walk!"

Instantly, the man was healed! He rolled up his sleeping mat and began walking!

The man probably had been there for years, waiting for someone to come to his aid. How many people had walked by and didn't see him, or chose not to see him. We have people all around us, every single day who we choose not to see. We need our vision changed in order to see these people and to really be the community and especially the body of Christ.

Probably one of the hardest things for us to do, is to put our personal feelings aside and humble ourselves and become a servant. That in fact is what Christ has called us to do.

During the pandemic that we are in the midst of during this writing, we have been asked to shelter at home and our economy has been literally shut down. We have been sked to lay down our personal desires to protect other people's wellbeing. We have been this way for over a month. There are people in the communities that are protesting having to stay home rather being free to do what they want to do including work to support their families. We are in a situation that we have not found ourselves ever before. I have found that my lifestyle has not really changed that much as I have been staying home most days and trying to keep myself busy. However, there are younger people whose lives have been turned upside down.

"But among you it will be different. Those who are the greatest among you should take the lowest rank, and the leader should be like a servant. Who is more important, the one who sits at the table or the one who serves? The one who sits at the table, of course. But not here! For I am among you as one who serves."

Luke 22:26-27, NLT

CHAPTER 6

Finding Our Giftedness

There is a point at which children and even adults cannot find fulfillment in expressing their giftedness within the family structure. The giftedness must be developed within a community. If there were no community there would be no motivation to express or develop our giftedness. Community begets giftedness. Community not only begets giftedness but brings fulfillment. Community creates a need for that giftedness.

As I write this portion of this book, I am sitting in a well-known coffee shop, really observing people as they sit eating and drinking their coffee and cold drinks, wondering what their stories may be. What is their giftedness? What do they do to serve the community? What need are they fulfilling for the community? Trash Collecting? Cooking? Building? Repairing cars? Serving someone's financial needs, as in banking or insurance, or financial planning. Many things that a family could not furnish within its framework. But clearly needed in the community. As my mind wonders, I think, I wonder what these people are struggling with. What are they anxious about? What are they happy about, as I hear laughter from one of the booths? I suddenly realize that within the community, nothing happens that does not have a ripple affect across the community. Our actions, our giftedness, our work, our recreation affects a multitude of people. I think of the saying from a sixteenth century poem, written by Donne, that has been incorporated in plays and movies, "No Man is An Island" The phrase expresses the idea that human beings do badly when isolated from others and need to be part of a community in order to thrive.

Donne was a Christian but this concept is shared by other religions. It is so true in every aspect of human behavior.

I truly believe that God created us to be in community. Part of God's character is that he is in relationship with the community of the trinity and wishes to be in community with us.

My mind goes back to when I was about a sophomore in high school, when I did the unthinkable. I needed to retrieve something out of my sister's bedroom. Anyone who has been a younger brother to an older sister knows that is like going into wardrobe closet and disappearing and never being heard from again. While I was in there, I noticed a card on her mirror which merely said, "I am Third". Later that evening, I fearfully mentioned to my sister, "What does, "I am third" mean? She looked up at me from the book she was reading, and looked at me with dagger eyes and after a few seconds, which felt like an eternity to me, and said. "It means God is first, others are second, and I am third" Then quickly continued, "What were you doing in my room?" Fortunately, I survived to write about it.

Serving others was meant to be done in community, not just within the family unit.

Another thing that happens in community is the raising up of leaders. Leaders seem to rise to the top in community. We can go back to the beginning in Genesis and see that God raised up leaders in the community of Israel. One of the things that I have noticed from reading the Old Testament is the fact that, when God raises up or calls someone to leadership there is a humility in that person even to the point that they do not feel qualified. Take Moses for example. He was to go to a fierce enemy and tell him to let the Nation of Israel go out of captivity. He did not feel qualified. God granted him the courage and the ability to accomplish what God had called him to do. I heard recently that Leaders do not raise up followers but more leaders.

The same is true for Abraham, Isaac and Jacob. Unfortunately for some the power goes to the head and they make mistakes along the way. I am sure that many of the prophets were reluctant to proclaim God's message to the nation of Israel Thankfully, they accepted God's call and were obedient.

There are many characteristics of a leader. Let me share a few leadership qualities that I believe are essential in good leadership. One, is vision. A leader must have a vision of where the group (community) needs to go to be the group it is called to be. He/she needs wisdom to know the steps to get there and organizational skill to organize the people to help get there.

Leaders need to have courage to, first, stay the course and secondly, to have courage enough to call the group back if they stray off the course. A leader needs courage to confront wrong in the group, which also means he/she must be, as the Apostle Paul says, above reproach. To live a pure and righteous life so as to not being reproach on themselves or the group.

A leader must be honest and ask forgiveness for wrong decisions and wrong behavior.

Many times in the history of our country God has called and raised up leaders to bring our country back to honoring God. Billy Graham comes immediately to mind. Also, Pat Roberson, and many of the preachers in our early years as a country. Read the book, "The Black Robed Regiment" by Dan Fisher to see what an influence the preachers of the founding fathers were to our country.[4]

At the time of the writing of this part of the book, our country is enduring watching the "leaders" of our country in the House of Representatives argue about the impeachment of our sitting president. The problem lies in the fact that many of those in leadership are trying to keep the power that they think they have instead of representing their constituents. However, the founding fathers set up our form of government to put checks and balances on the three parts of our government. That being the Legislature, Executive, and Judicial.

Fortunately, our founding fathers divided the leadership in the legislative branch of our country into two sections. Bills or prospective laws including impeachment must pass in both sections and houses. So the House of Representatives acts as a check against the Senate and the Senate acts as a check on the House.

COMMUNITY WITHOUT GOD IS JUST A CROWD!!

SECTION III
The Church

CHAPTER 7

The Beginnings

The problem with the church is twofold. One, we must, as, Christians, speak with grace. The scriptures emphasize that there is no one that is perfect, and everyone has some kind of sin that we must deal with and sometimes battle on a daily basis. The second, is to speak up when there is wrong being done in our world and specifically in our nation.

Specifically, where was the church when Madilyn Murray O'Hare lobbied to get prayer and the Bible out of our public education system. Where is the church even now, when thousands of unborn babies are being killed on a daily basis? I know that there is a delicate balance that we need to walk in condemning the sin and loving the sinner. Much about this later in the book.

We send missionaries all over the world in hopes that the Christian belief and life is better for them than what they have. We believe the Christian experience is the answer to their life's problems. We become passionate about reaching them.

However, we shrink down when it becomes obvious that what our own country has is not what we envision our lives being. Where is our passion to convert our country to Christian morality? Our tolerance has become the nail in Christianity's coffin.

I fear that there are too many of the Christian faith that do not know what they believe or are not totally convinced that it is THE truth. I believe that there are those of the Christian faith that believe it is the answer for their lives but are not convinced that it will be for everybody.

In this modern society that we live in it is imperative that our faith be so sound and solid that we believe that it is the answer for everybody on this planet.

I am convinced that many of our mega churches are a mile wide (in other words, a weekend throng of thousands) but an inch deep (in other words, not very sound and solid in faith or doctrine.)

This is the problem we have with the Muslim faith as they believe so strongly that they have the answer for everyone's life that they are willing to do anything to convert someone even by force. I am not saying that. As Christians, we need to go out and start killing people that do not believe in Christ and His redemptive work on the cross and resurrection. But we can be more aggressive in showing our experience that Jesus Christ came to provide life to us that we would never experience otherwise.

I suppose that there are a lot of different ideas about what a true Christian is. I believe that a Christian is a person who has come to realize that Christ was alive on this earth and went to the cross to take our place for the sins that we have committed. It's also a person that believes that trusting Christ for everything in life has to be the only way to have a successful life. I have gone through a lot of troubles and I don't know how I would made it through if I did not think that God through his Holy Spirit had walked with me through it. Because He is my foundation, He became my fulcrum to get through every struggle.

My intentions are not to bore you with a repeat of a thesis on church history but to share with you what I think the real intentions of the creator of what the church was to be from its beginnings."

I suppose the church actually began with Adam and Eve as they, "walked with God in the cool of the evening."

We see the nation of Israel in the best of conditions and the worst of conditions. They were obedient at times and disobedient at times, but the fact of the matter is that they never ceased to be the people of God, Jehovah.

Let me say I believe the primary purpose of the church is for taking care of the widows and orphans. In other words, taking care of people's physical needs, food, shelter, clothing or what our modern-day world thinks of as Welfare.

Often as I have studied and guided churches through the process of developing a mission statement, trying to define what we are to be doing as a group of called out believers that it is imperative to keep that statement and ideas in front of the congregation many times over the course of years or decades. We as humans and even Christians tend to forget that which we do not see consistently in front of us. The same is true, that which our founding fathers brought together in the Declaration of Independence and our Constitution of our great country will soon be forgotten, if our schools and media and leaders do not constantly reiterate.

I fear that there are too many of the Christians faith that do not know what they believe or are not totally convinced that it is the truth. I think that there are those of the Christian faith that believe it is the answer for their lives but are not convinced that it will be for everybody.

In this modern society that we live in it is imperative that our faith be so sound and solid that we believe that it is the answer for everybody on the planet.

Whenever I confront Christians about getting involved in changing the community or the country for that matter, I almost always get the answer something like this, "My hope is in Christ" It is good to have a hope based on Christ but I think He would tell us to make that hope an active one in this life. This really concerns me in the family of Christ. Our faith has to be a right now faith not just a faith in life in the hereafter. Christ sent the disciples out to make a difference in their world. The scriptures tell us that they turned the world upside down.

If we want to corrupt any kind of action, give the responsibility to the government.

Let me explain, this with a personal experience. While in between pastorates I worked for the Salvation Army in a large metropolitan city in our country, as Director of Social Services. My days were spent interviewing people or families who came to us for financial help in the form of rent assistance, food, utility bills assistance and for the homeless a place to stay. I had an extensive budget for this and seldom did I turn people away without helping them. However, there were times when I ran out of funds and had to turn people to other assistance programs.

I was usually notified by the Department of Human Services (government) if they found someone of committing welfare fraud and to watch out for them.

Years later, I worked for the Department of Social Services (government) in another large metropolitan city in a primary black area, helping people receive food stamps and medical coverage, and Day Care assistance for their children. I was employed there for about 6 months. That was about all I could take of their political insaneness. We had a man, who was in his early fifties, who was the office trainer. He had been there for 19 years and had interviewed for a supervisor position and had never been offered that position. The Supervisors were primarily black females and this man was white. I always thought this was a little strange. He knew more about regulations and the social service system then all the supervisors in the office combined. I asked this gentleman a curious question during my training: What happens when we run out of funds? He looked at me with this strange look on his face and said, "What do you mean?" I said, "What happens when someone comes in for assistance and we have no money in the Social Service budget?" He responded, "That has never happened. If they come in for assistance and meet all the criteria and all their information checks out, then, by law, we have to assist them." I guess the government can just print more money to pay the vendors.

Basically, whatever the government does, it does poorly. This is just as true of the Department of Human services. Part of the reason is that government means bureaucrats spending someone else's money. Naturally they are prolific with it; it's not their money. Besides, they are not subject to market forces—consequently, there is no "bottom line." Private investors who make bad decisions get punished for them; bureaucrats who make bad decisions suffer no such consequences. Private initiatives that don't work get canceled, but with very few exceptions.

Let me illustrate this by sharing a fictional situation. Let's say I am eating a sack of food from some fast food restaurant. You come along and state that you are hungry and if I could share a bit of my lunch, you would be grateful. So, I share my lunch with you. Now, I feel good as I have shown concern and compassion on you. You feel grateful for the food and perhaps some time in the future, you show someone the same compassion. It's a win, win for everyone.

Now let's say that it's the same situation, except the governor comes along and puts a gun to my head and orders me to share my lunch with you. So I share my lunch with you and we both have something to eat. However, there is no morality in this situation because I was forced to give you part of my lunch. I have no feelings of compassion or concern because I was forced to share. You, on the other hand, do not feel gratitude, but instead feel entitled because I had a whole lunch which I worked for and you only get a portion of a lunch, which you did not work for. Another outcome of this is that we look at the actions of the governor as being admired but if he had been a private citizen, would have been arrested for assault and extortion.

I share that to show how the Department of Human Services operates as opposed to how charitable organizations such as the church would change the mindset of taking care of the less fortunate.

Back in early America, neighbors would help neighbors in times of need, whether it be to raise a barn or harvest crops or sickness, or loss of jobs. That sort of kindness and care has literally disappeared in America today with our six-foot fence's around our house, and automatic garage door openers. We can go for months and not even see our neighbors. Remember the illustration of pointing the finger at someone and three pointing back at you. Guilty! During those times in America, it was the church that was the center of activities and relationships. That should be the case even today. The Government and our Education system believe that the center of community activities should be our schools. That is so they can control not only what happens but how we think and how we interact.

Most Americans think that economic conservatives, political conservatives, and highly successful people do not care about poor and needy. In most cases this is simply not true. The responsibility for providing assistance to the needy must not be left to the government because the only resources the government has, has been taken from those who have earned it. Not surprising to me is that more of our charity goes to the poor through religious organizations than secular or government programs. Case in point, the Salvation Army programs, as stated earlier benefits more people per dollar than any government programs.

Here are some interesting statistics given by the Heritage Foundation in a 2011 report. 92 percent of Americas poor have a microwave oven, 80 percent have air conditioning, 66 percent have a DVD player and Cable or Satellite TV, and nearly 75 percent have at least one car or truck. In addition, 96 percent of "poor" parents stated that their children never went hungry at any time during the year due to lack of money. In any third world country a person with these possessions would be undeniably rich.

The government becomes the noose that strangles the golden goose by overreaching control.

When people are taught to look to government or to others to care for them, they will not look to God, Jehovah. God must be our source. The prophet Jeremiah said, "Cursed is man who trust in mankind" (Jeremiah 17:5) When people in trouble are led or encouraged to look to politicians and the federal government for help, they will not seek God and find the real assistance they desperately need. When "we the people" are taught not to love, care for, or assist our neighbor, we to, have been deceived and contribute to loss of freedom and that kind of living leads to the loss of hope for many.

Because of these kinds of actions by the government, the government becomes a God. Mostly because it takes care of the poor and gives them a good life that is void of hard work or any kind of morality. Therefore big government will do everything that people have a right to like abortion or whatever they deem to be good. They make everyone equal. I am not a person who can think for himself. I am just a number for Social Security purposes or in most politicians minds, another vote. Big government gives people safety at the cost of freedom.

It's amazing to me that our country has been slaughtering its citizens, much like the holocaust through making abortion legal and easy to obtain. The church sits idly by and allows it to happen. How have we allowed this to happen?

I think the biggest lie that the church has taken in is the misinterpretation of' "separation of Church and State."

The thought invading the church today is that they should not be involved in politics and the government. I believe that this is the reason that our country is in such a deep moral decline, and our government, nationally and locally is so corrupt.

James Robinson, in his book, "The Stream", has this to say about the church,

> It is because the transforming resurrection power of
> Christ has been replaced with mere religious consent of

church membership. It is obvious Christians have not
been leading people to Christ. Their witness is weak or
missing. Unless hearts are changed, and minds renewed
by the Holy Spirit, people will not think right or live right.
Most professing Christians don't vote. If they did and vote
on biblical principles, we would not be on our present
disastrous course because Christians are by far the largest
identifiable percentage of the population.

I believe it was President Lyndon Johnson who changed the tax code
to read, "Non-profit entities, including churches cannot 'participate in',
or intervene in (including the publishing or distributing of statements),
any political campaign on behalf of (or in opposition to) any candidate
for public office." This law has been on the books since the early 60's. It is
also unconstitutional.

This law goes completely contrary to the First Amendment to the
Constitution which states, "Congress shall make no law respecting an
establishment of religion or prohibiting the free exercise thereof; or
abridging the freedom of speech, or of the press, or the right of the people
peaceably to assemble, and to petition the Government for a redress of
grievances."

The church has used this unconstitutional tax code to tie their hands
to influence our country for the good.

If the church believes it should not be involved in politics and
government, why does each church put itself under the authority of the
government by incorporating... I know most churches if not all, do it in
order to be recognized as a non-profit corporation to receive funds that
are tax deductible. I always wonder how the giving to the church would
be affected if their gifts were not tax deductibles, Biblical based followers
should not be affected in the least. Scripture says to bring all the tithes into
the store house of God (Malachi 3:10)

An attorney for the Christian Law Association, said in a conference
I once attended that there was a case against a Christian School that was
sponsored by a church. The argument for the School was that they were
not under the control of the government and could teach the Bible. The
State attorney asked the Pastor if the church was incorporated. His reply

was, "Yes we are incorporated" The attorney for the state then stated, "Then you have placed yourself under our authority. The state (government) won their case.

Pastors and church boards are so concerned that they will lose their nonprofit status that they are scared to speak out on subjects that pertain to our government and politics and so they don't speak out. If they would only realize that they have a constitutional right to speak out.

God will not hold us guiltless. Not to speak is to speak. Not to act is to act."

I heard a story a few years ago about the Gladiators in the arenas back 40 AD where Pompeii would put the gladiators in the area and release a whole heard of elephants. The gladiators would begin to throw their spears at the elephants and killing many of them. Suddenly the elephants realized what was happening to the heard and begin to let out a loud cry all at the same time. The audience who at the beginning were desiring to see the gladiators win and kill all of the elephants. Suddenly the audience turned and began to cheer for the elephants. The sound of the elephants crying changed the whole atmosphere in that arena.

I really believe that the church, Christian people has sit back and allowed many things to be changed in our country. In 1964 when Lyndon Johnson made a law that if any nonprofit speaks out for any political candidate, their nonprofit status would be withdrawn. In 1972 when prayer was taken out of public education the church stood by and allowed that to happen. The same when abortion began to recognized as legal, when some states have legalized same sex marriages. The church has sit back and said nothing and continued to have their prayer meetings and pot-luck dinners, I believe that it is time, like the elephants need to begin to let out a cry and change our culture in America, Recently, we have allowed the government to shut down our church services because of a virus. It appears that we no longer believe in God's protection and divine healing. Wake Up church! I am reminded of the hymn we used to sing frequently in church, "The Battle Hymn of the Republic'

I believe the body of Christ has lost some of its strength and vision for what the body of believers can accomplish in our country. We have gone back into our prayer closets and let the world turn out however it does because we have an eternal home. While we are here, we are to make a difference. The Lord's Prayer says "Thy Kingdom come here on earth as it is in heaven. We are not operating like the first century church did.

They turned the world upside down, just like those elephants did. Joshua marched around Jericho seven times and gave a loud shout and the walls came down. It's time for the church to raise up and give a loud shout so the walls of evil in our country come tumbling down.

"First they came for the communists, and I did not speak out because I was not a communist; Then they came for the trade unionists, and I did not speak out because I was not a trade unionist; Then they came for the Jews, and I did not speak out because I was not a Jew; Then they came for me and there was no one left to speak out for me." Martin Niemoller

John Quincy Adams said, "The greatest glory of the American Revolution was that it bound together in one indissoluble bond the principles of Christianity and the principles of civil government"

Apparently, Mr. Adams had no problem of mixing church and state.

Samuel Johnson said this, "Remember, too, that you are the redeemed of the Lord that you are bought with a price, even the inestimable price of the precious blood of the Son of God. . . Acquaint yourselves with Him in His word and holy ordinances."

John Witherspoon, one of the revolution pastors, said, "Had the (founding fathers), during the revolution, a suspicion of any attempt to war against Christianity, that Revolution would have been strangled in its cradle. ...At the time of the adoption of the constitution and its amendments, the universal sentiment was that Christianity should be encouraged...In this age, there is no substitute for Christianity ...That was the religion of the founders of the republic and they expected it to remain the religion of their descendants."

Witherspoon also said, in regard to pastors preaching on politics and the revolution, and also being involved in its active resolution, "Why is he deprived of this right? Is it by offense or disqualification? Is it a sin against the public to become a minister? Does it merit that the person, who is guilty of it should be immediately deprived of one of his most important rights as a citizen? ...is a minister then disqualified for the office of senator or representative?"

One of the great revolution pastors who gave his life for it is quoted as saying, "I am a clergyman, it is true, but I am a member of society as well as the poorest layman, and my liberty is as dear to me as to any man. Shall I then sit still, and enjoy myself at home, when the best blood of the continent is spilling? Heaven forbid it! ...Do you think, If America should be conquered, I should be safe? Far from it. And would you not sooner fight like a man than die like a dog? I am called by my country to its defense. The cause is just and noble. ...and so far, am I from thinking that I am wrong. I am convinced it is my duty so to do, a duty I owe to my God and to my country."

The church must return to its original purpose, "the great commission" Matthew 28:18-20.

> I have been given all authority in heaven and on earth. Therefore, go and make disciples of all nations, baptizing them in the name of the Father and the Son and the Holy Spirit. Teach these new disciples to obey all the commands I have given you. And be sure of this: I am with you always, even to the end of the age.

I suppose it could be called proselytizing, but the church, the body of Christ, must make its message to bring people into the kingdom not another church or body or denomination.

In a paper published in 2008 by the "Forerunner" about the Asbury Revival that broke out in 1970 at the Asbury College shares a quote from David McKenna saying that another revival will breakout soon and probably on a college campus because he sees signs. He says:

> "Those signs include a generation of students wounded by family breakdowns and searching for spiritual fulfillment. Much of the coming revival will be a delayed reaction." McKenna thinks to what happened at Asbury College 48 years ago will happen again.

Someone has said that Revivals often occur in times of discord. In this day of age, we can hardly imagine a time of greater discord in America. People are at odds with each other spiritually, emotionally, relationally, politically, almost in every area of our lives there is discord.

Let's look at the word of God, as a tool to teach us what the purpose of the church is in our society or any society for that matter.

> One day the widow of a member of the group of prophets came to Elisha and cried out, "My husband who served you is dead and you know how he feared the Lord. But now a creditor has come, threatening to take my two sons as slaves.

II Kings 4:1 (NLT)

Elisha was the protégé and successor of the great prophet Elijah. They served the nation of Israel as spiritual leaders during a dark period in the wake of King Solomon's reign, when the kingdom had been split into two and weakened buy a series of bad kings. Once a mighty and unified nation, Israel was now the object of frequent invasions from foreign armies.

Though they were both heroic men of God and their names were similar, Elijah battled a king and the priests of Baal in Spectacular confrontations of spiritual power. He separated himself from everyday folks and preached fiery messages of judgment that demanded repentance.

Elisha, on the other hand, lived among the common people. He made it his business to hang with down-and-out folks. As a preacher, his primary message was one of grace, mercy, and hope. So, it was not unusual for a poor, distraught woman to come to him in search of assistance.

I believe that the priests of the 21st century, our pastors/teachers, are much like Elisha. They try to live with the common people and be counselor, compassionate friend to those under their care. However, I predict that the Lord will raise up another Elijah who will call our world, country, and church to repentance. I really see, in our country and the world, a need to bring people to repentance and accountability. We hear a lot today in the church about accountability partners to lean on so that we are not tempted to sin. I really think that the church has lost its power to redeem people through proclaiming the name of Jesus and the power that He has in people's lives.

This "certain woman" here in II Kings is a widow. This particular widow's late husband was apparently one of Elisha's associate prophets.

Then, like today, ministry was not a lucrative career, so this prophet's family was already poor. His death simply plunged the family into deeper financial crises.

Certainly, the widow's husband was not expecting to die before paying off his debt. But he did, leaving the burden to his family. Today, one would hopefully have life insurance and a will in place to ensure the financial stability of the family. That was not an option for this man.

In those days, the taking and selling of children was a legal means of collecting on a debt. And since mercy did not seem to be in the heart of the widow's creditor, her two sons were in danger of being taken as payment for the family's outstanding debt. In desperation she goes to Elisha, who had been her late husband's boss in the ministry.

It is important to note that his woman had the kind of faith to believe that whatever trouble she was in financially, God could work it out. She didn't go to the bank; she went to the man of God. She didn't go to the pawnshop; she went to the man of God. Playing the state lottery never occurred to this woman. Some of us, however, are looking for worldly solutions before seeking biblical solutions. I am afraid the church is guilty of the same mistake, in relying on government to do the job they are called to do by the head of the church himself, Jesus Christ.

As a pastor, I had many people, inside my church, and outside, come to me for assistance. I did not have the resources, myself to help, but on some occasions the church had a small amount of funds to aid people. I will address this problem later in this book.

"What can I do to help you?" Elisha asked. "Tell me, what do you have in the house?"

"Nothing at all, except a flask of olive oil," she replied.

And Elisha said, "Borrow as many empty jars as you can from your friends and neighbors. Then go into your house with your sons and shut the door behind you. Pour olive oil from your flask into the jars, setting each one aside when it is filled."

So, she did as she was told. Her sons kept bringing jars to her and she filled one after another. Soon every container was full to the brim!

"Bring me another jar." She said to one of her sons.

"There aren't any more!" he told her. And then the olive oil stopped flowing.

II Kings 4:2--6

God expects us to use the resources that are available to us in our house. If Elisha would be here today, he might be telling the widow, "Have a garage sale" or at least asking the same question, "What do you have in your house?"

Pure and genuine religion in the sight of God the Father means caring for orphans and widows in their distress and refusing to let the world corrupt you.

James 1:27

James tells us the real purpose of the church. Not only to evangelize the world but to take care of people in their distress.

Let me say several things about the previous verse. First of all, the church should be about a relationship with their God and other people and not about a "religion", but the fact remains that we are not doing what scripture has said we are supposed to be doing. Secondly, we have allowed the world to corrupt the church and thus are assigned duties, taking care of widows and orphans.

When we begin to think about the church, we think intrinsically of something "out there" or in other words, an abstract thing. We think, "The church needs to do this, or the church needs to be more aggressive or more evangelical or more loving. When in reality, we are the church. So, in effect, the church is speaking to itself.

I think what made the church so powerful and effective in the first century in Acts is the fact that it was not wrapped up in a building. (Acts 2:41)

> Those who believed what Peter said were baptized and added to the church that day—about 3,000 in all

There are so many church buildings that stand empty 5-6 days a week and thousands of dollars being wasted in a building, when much of that could be aiding the poor.

During our current pandemic with a virus that originated in China, our country has basically been shut down, including churches. We are not allowed to gather in groups larger than 10. So many churches have held their worship services by streaming over the internet. This has almost eliminated the need for large buildings. I am not sure what will happen when the pandemic passes and we are allowed to gather to worship together. I am thinking people will get used to doing worship in their pajamas.

According to, "Lift the Vote.org,"

17 million Evangelical Christians were either not registered to vote or did not vote. 26% of eligible votes are Evangelical Christians or 52 million. In 2008 and 2012 only 63% (33 million) voted.

George Washington wrote, in agreement with Alexander Hamilton,

> Whereas it is the particular duty of the Executive branch, "to take care that the laws be faithfully executed... the permanent interests and happiness of the people require that every legal and necessary step should pursue to avoid violent and unwarrantable proceedings.

I have thought a lot about the church and what it is supposed to look like in our modern society. The church has splintered into hundreds of different branches. When I mention the church in this section, I will be referring to the total body of Christ in this world. I will refer to the total church rather than to one particular faction.

Let's look at the beginning of the church as it is created in the book of Acts.

"On the day of Pentecost, all the believers were meeting together in one place. Suddenly, there was a sound from heaven like the roaring of a mighty windstorm, and it filled the house where they were sitting. Then what looked like flames of tongues of fire appeared and settled on each of them. And everyone present was filled with the Holy Spirit and began speaking in other languages as the Holy Spirit gave this ability." Acts 2:1--4

Then moving down in the narrative to verses 42-45.

"All the believers devoted themselves to the apostles' teaching, and to fellowship, and to sharing in meals (including the Lord's Supper), and to prayer.

A deep sense of awe came over them all, and the apostles performed many miraculous signs and wonders. And all the believers met together in one place and shared everything they had. They sold their property and possessions and shared the money with those in need."

This was the first of churches welfare program. It is interesting to note that once the Holy Spirit came, the desire to share their possessions came with it.

I am reminded of Peter's admonishing the church in I Peter 3:8,

Finally, all of you should be on one mind. Sympathize with each other. Love each other as brothers and sisters. Be tender-hearted and keep a humble attitude.

As I was working with a new church plant in Oklahoma, a tornado came through and devastated the city. A group of people from the church walked through the ruble and whenever they came upon someone going through the ruble that was once there home, they would ask them what they needed, and they would write a check right then and there and told them to go get whatever they needed, and some were taken to the stores. They provided almost $200,000. Worth of assistance that first week or so.

One of the reasons they could do that was they did not own a building but were renting facilities in a college. It seems that we have things turned upside down in the church today. We are so focused on buildings that we cannot see the real purpose of the church.

Many of the millennial generation have been turned off by the church because of the church's lack of integrity and transparency and judge mentalism.

When I was in High School, my father was transferred from Kansas City to Salt Lake City. My high school years were full of learning about the Church of Jesus Christ of Latter-day Saints church. Otherwise known as the Mormon Church. I do not agree with a lot or most of their doctrine, but they have the most sophisticated Welfare programs in the world. If you are a part of the Mormon Church, you will never go hungry or live on the streets. Every family in the Mormon Church is responsible for five other families within the church. They are to visit each of their families once a month and make sure they do not go hungry and if they are on the verge of being homeless, the church will provide meals and housing assistance. The organizational structure of the church, as I understand it, is each congregation is called a "Ward". Several Wards make up a "Stake" Each Stake has a building in which 2-4 Wards meet in. Each Stake will join other Stake's to build a Stake Farm. Each family is responsible to work on the farm a certain number of hours a month. This farm will supply the food assistance for a number of families that the church provides for. The church buildings are always paid for before any services are held in the building. They have no paid clergy within the congregations. Each Stake has their leader and each ward has their lay pastor which, I believe is called the lead Elder. Each family in each Ward is required to tithe. If the tithe is not paid, someone will be knocking on your door. Part of their doctrine is that you move up in the Heavens depending on how much work you do here. It is a very legalistic doctrine and based primarily on works and not grace. But their way of addressing poverty and assisting people's needs should be commended and perhaps copied.

The primary purpose of the church is to bring people into a redeeming relationship with God, the creator. When people become transformed into faithful followers of Jesus Christ they naturally turn from being selfish thinking to being servants and mindful of the needs of others.

The younger generations have become what some have called, "the entitlement generation". In other words, they have the mindset that they have the right to have their needs met and in a lot of cases even their desires met.

As the church, (believers) convert and lead others to trust Jesus Christ for their fulfillment in their lives, they will turn from being selfish to becoming servants and begin to fill the purpose of the "church" providing for the widows and orphans and other social needs.

I believe we need to begin to think in terms of "widows and orphans" as single parents and children in single parent homes. Since the divorce rate is becoming alarmingly close to 60%, the caring for these broken families becomes the acute need in our generation.

Alexis de Tocqueville, an aristocrat who traveled in America in the early nineteenth century is quoted as saying, "It was never assumed in the United States that the citizen of a free country has a right to do whatever he pleases. Americans, however, derive their obligations not from government mandate but from religious morality and social pressure. There are unsurmountable sects in America, but "all sects preach the same moral law in the name of God."

"Moreover, religion balances entrepreneurial striving; the latter teaches how to better yourself, for your own good, while the former teaches obligations to others for the good of the community. Therefore, quite apart from its theological function, Tocquiville, writes that for Americans, religion "must be regarded as the first of their political institutions. Tocquiville sees "rights" as steering people to do what is right—for him, the free society is also the decent society in which people can simultaneously do good and do well.

Everywhere in America, Tocquiville, upon visiting our country is struck by how Americans look to themselves rather than the government to get things done. Initially, people try to do things themselves. If they can't they rely on family. (Tocquiville notes that from the outset it was families, not individuals, who settled America. Americans also employ what Tocquiville calls "the principle of association" to form committees, voluntary groups—religious groups, recreational groups, philanthropic groups, educational institutions and so on.

Unlike in Europe, Tocquiville observes that in America, "when a private individual meditates an understanding, however directly connected it may be with the welfare of society, he never thinks of soliciting the cooperation of the government; but he publishes his plan, offers to execute it, courts the assistance of other individuals, and struggles manfully against all obstacles…in the end, the sum of these private undertakings far exceeds all that the government could have done.

This sounds so unfamiliar to our modern-day mindset, doesn't it? The bigger government gets, the more we tend to rely on the government to do things for us. And the cycle keeps repeating itself. Right?

Tocqueville finds the same participatory spirit when it comes to democracy—the people get involved. Their involvement, however is most active and effective at the local level. This is the spirit of the New England town meetings. Democracy works well here because people know their own problems and how best to solve them. Tocquiville takes a different view of the federal government. He terms it, "an immense and tutelary power" which seeks to control people by promising "to secure their gratifications and to watch over their fate."

Its power may seem mild at first, but it could gradually expand until it becomes, "absolute". It promises are illusionary. "It would be like the authority of a parent if…its object was to prepare men for manhood; but it seeks on the contrary to keep them in perpetual childhood." In sum, an overreaching federal government would make itself the provider and arbiter of the happiness of Americans, but what it would really do is "to spare them all care of thinking and all trouble of living.

I think the founding fathers never intended for the government to intrude on people's lives as it does in the twenty-first century. When America was being settled people took it upon themselves to get things done. They were pretty efficient at it too. As time went on, people began to rely on government to get things done. I believe it began at least in a great degree during the great depression in the nineteen thirties.

James Robison in his book, "The Stream" says this about the early church, "I don't know if the early church strategized to transform the empire of Rome. We have scant evidence of such. They were more obviously enamored with being a part of a new nation that came from heaven, filled them with the love of God, and empowered them with the same spirit who raised Jesus from death. The early church infiltrated Rome and affected the known world like leaven invades a whole lump of dough. It was and is the kingdom of God. This kingdom is still the only God nations."

These people who believed in the power that was at their disposal, somehow knew that the love they had received from God was more powerful than political kingdoms, tyrants and death. We have little or no evidence that the early church had a preconceived strategy for changing the world or infiltrating their society.

Robinson goes on later to say this:

"Whenever issues of national and moral importance (which have now been made political) are addressed by a religious leader, we hear the outcry, "Stay out of politics". In other words, they say ministers must avoid real-life issues, problems, and challenges on the national stage by never standing up with hopeful, helpful solutions. The truth is, Christians, all people of faith, and certainly preachers of the Word of God are obligated to speak out and to stand for their convictions. People with a secular, humanist, God-denying founding documents are continually organizing in every community. They force their views on the population through protests and radical political activities while never giving up an inch of their sacred turf, however unsacred it actually is. They expect the church community to shut up and go back to sleep and keep our faith to ourselves."[32]

Any time I try, as a minister to address a social or moral issue that is in the news, I hear comments, like, "Larry, You need to stay out of politics" or "You need to stick to spiritual issues". When people respond that way, I want to lose my Christianity for a moment. When some political figure speaks about the church or Christian people, no one says to them, "You need to stay out of Spiritual things. During our pandemic, some of the leaders in government have said churches must close but bars and liquor stores can be open, then they are messing with my constitutional rights and freedoms. I also have the constitutional right to speak about the biblical values that ought to be followed.

As an ordained minister, I have had people ask me, "Larry, are you getting to political?" I am really not sure what that means. I love God and the church, and people. I am concerned that Christians are not making a difference in this world and especially in America. The New Testament church set the known world upside down and it seems that the church today is barely existing. There must be a way to right the ship, so to speak.

Our founding fathers never conceived a nation separated from God. We have a move on today to separate God from government, and God from society. That is not why America was founded. America is built on God. When America divorces from God, she will fall more violently then Humpty Dumpty.

Religion is strong enough to make men hate one another, but it is not strong enough to make men love one another. God is calling us to a life filled with the power of transforming love and the boldness of New Testament believers to stand against the powers of this present darkness. When God rules in individual lives sound principles will prevail in our land.

When I begin to think about the church and how we are to love, I begin to think about the word Tolerance. Maybe the idea of Tolerating a life style or just the idea of ideology. When does love for a person blend into tolerance of a life style. I am afraid that the church or we as Christians begin to tolerate something when we should stand up against it and still be able to express love towards a person.

There is no freedom apart from God and the acceptance of personal responsibility. There can be no effective government without responsible citizens living under moral order. The question is, whose morality we are going to accept and live under. The founding father's intention and encouraged the morality of God's divine word was the morality that was the only morality that would be able to guide a free society. We are in the process of forfeiting the freedom our founders established—a freedom built on moral absolutes and a strong, but limited, government. Contrary to popular opinion, the American founders believed that everyone has a general knowledge of natural moral law and divine providence. Supernatural wisdom and direction is our only hope.

We, as Christians have silently allowed the termination of more than fifty million innocent lives in the wombs of their mothers. Hitler murdered over eleven million people in the Holocaust, and Stalin almost twenty million. America has doubled that, and the church has set idly by and allowed it to happen. And it continues.

Abraham Lincoln in his first inaugural address, said, "Intelligence, patriotism, Christianity, and a firm reliance on Him who has never yet forsaken this favored land, are still competent to adjust, in the best way, all our present difficulty."

Today's unhealthy sense of entitlement and expectation, along with the demand to be cared for by the government while continually building hate for the other person because they have more is simply evil.

Now is the time to pray without ceasing for God to bring His people together in heart-harmony and for our leaders to come and reason together with the same dedication, determination and unity of purpose that has exposed the terrorist of our time.

We as pastors must come together to sound the trumpet of love and peace, no matter what denomination or faith. Our unity will show the world that we can get along and love. We must set the example to Christians around the world.

We must pray for another God-breathed revival in our country such as happened back in the early seventies at Asbury College.

One of our biggest problems with our governmental systems in America is that instead of our leaders doing the right things to keep our country free they continue to protect their turf. They make decisions not on their eye on the next thing but on the next election.

I am reminded of a poster I saw in one of my classrooms:

1) Evil is real
2) Ideas have consequences
3) We are spiritual beings
4) The majority is not always right. History—both secular and biblical—demonstrates that "popular" is not the same as "just." Democracy without responsible, principled, self-governing citizens

will lead to mobocracy. Laws must be based on something firmer than the blowing winds of public opinion.

5) Truth withstands debate

6) People matter most.

7) Equality is not sameness.

8) If government does not serve, it will enslave...When society depends on government for sustenance, the people fall into bondage. Government has nothing it does not first take from its citizens.

9) Truth has a source."

Please hear my heart concerning our nation and the poor. America's poor and needy are being hurt and held back by bad policies and practices on the part of our own government.

What President Lyndon B. Johnson launched, back in the sixties, as a war on poverty has proven to be a war on the poor that actually keeps many not only poor but hopelessly enslaved as dependents with little or no confidence or meaningful ambition. The pitiful plight of the needy has made them the pawns of politicians who need their votes to retain their power. This practice is not only insane; it is cruel and will cripple America economically."

It has long been my impression that the church has neglected their responsibility to preserve our freedoms in America. We, (the church and especially the clergy) have swallowed the lie that the phrase, "separation of church and state", which is not in the constitution, means we cannot say or do anything that pertains to government or politics. Which is totally the opposite of the churches responsibility when it comes to our freedoms.

We, as the church must become well informed and actively involved in the political process. Christians, pastors, and church leaders must totally reject the lie that, "separation of church and state" means that people of faith, must remain silent, uninformed, and uninvolved. If we who recognize truth and stand for it can turn the tide in America. Our nation's founders knew that the limits of the constitution were placed on the government, not on the people or religion.

I once heard someone define the word, "expert" this way: An "X" is a mathematical term for the unknown, and a "spurt" is a drip of liquid under pressure. So, an expert is "an unknown drip under pressure".[33]

So, I ask this question in each of the areas in our discussion, who determines that these guardians are experts? Indeed, what makes them more expert, and all that may or may not entail, than those who operate in the private sector? Are the latter not the true experts by experience, training, and knowledge?"

We don't usually associate the word, "politics" with the church. Although in many church bodies, communities, there is plenty of politicking going on. Back in the early Greek and Roman culture, the word for church was "ekklesia". It was also used to mean a secular institution operating in the marketplace in a governmental capacity. I really believe that the "ekklesia" needs to have an influence in the marketplace.

Being consistent with our new nature we are to bring His government into this world's government by our presence in focused agreement.

I think that many times that we forget the prayer that Christ taught the disciples when he said,

> Our Father in heaven, may your name be kept holy. May your kingdom come soon. May your will be done on earth as it is in heaven...

We forget that we are not just to sit back and wait for the kingdom to come to us, but we are to create his kingdom here on earth by creating an atmosphere of unconditional love, by affecting the culture in government and community.

I think this is totally why our founding fathers envisioned a country, a nation that based on a Constitution that encapsulates the "ekklesia" influencing the government to make righteous decision based on the government of God's kingdom.

CHAPTER 8

Modern Churchianity

I am not going to get into a long discourse on theology, but I would like to share what I believe has been the problem with our churches for many years.

Through the 50's and 60's and into the 80's and 90's the church has been about following rules to have a relationship with the heavenly Father. So being the imperfect human beings that we are, we followed the rules and gave everyone the impressions that the relationship was there and was okay.

Now in the 2000's the pendulum has swung to the other extreme and the thought has been that God loves us no matter what we do so rules do not matter. That is the reason that promiscuity and divorce is about the same in the church as in the secular world.

The truth probably is somewhere in the middle. The rules still matter but they are forgivable, and lives are redeemable, and we can have a close relationship with the Father if we desire it.

The story of the woman in scripture caught in adultery and brought before the Lord may shed some light on this subject. The woman was brought before the religious leaders and Christ and ask him what they should do. Jesus Christ said, "He without sin cast the first stone." The fact was that Jesus was the only one present that could have cast a stone, but he did not. After everyone dropped their stones and left, Christ asked her where her accusers were. Gone! He says, "Neither do I condemn you." The only one that could have condemned her chose not to. Then he does something that proves His divinity. He says, "Go and sin no more."

First of all, he recognizes her sin. He calls it a sin and let her know it (the rules) is wrong. Then he gives her a command, "Sin no more." In other words, choose to follow me and my love will go with you. As I read scripture, God always gives a promise after a command. There is the transforming power indwelt within a person.

For some reason, we Christians think that another person's sins are worse than ours. We point our fingers at those who drink, or smoke or are promiscuous and think "Well, I don't do those things, so I am okay." Scripture says in Romans 6:23 that, "the wages of sin (no matter what it is) is death." Simply the act of pointing our finger and judging another person is sin. Right? The good thing is that, "For by grace you have been saved." Your sin, the other person's sin is already forgiven because of the cross.

People seek the wrong answers by establishing the wrong King and in so doing miss the necessary relationship with the Father.

My experience with my own earthly father was mixed. My father was an excellent provider for me and our family. He made good money as an executive in a large company. Because of that I do not find it hard to believe that my heavenly father will take care of me and my family even though I have never made much money.

However, my father was not very expressive in showing me or any of my siblings love. Also, he was not a good positive person and rarely had any good things to say about his children. Because of this, I did not have a good self-image and confidence. Because of this I find it hard to believe God loves me and that I have His approval for who I am and what I do.

Part of the problem in our immoral society is that many of us have not had good moral examples to follow. Scripture says that "The sins of the father will be visited unto the third and fourth generation/" (Numbers 14:18). Certainly, this is true in many families.

We have entered into an unpresented time in our country. Along with dealing with a worldwide pandemic, we are dealing with some race issues that have created demonstration and riots in the streets of most cities across our country. The demonstrations have come under the banner of "Black Lives Matter". However what we need is the concern for life itself. The idea that one life matters more than another is absurd. Christ died for all.

All men, and women of all races were created in the image of God.

His word tells us that each one of us is more valuable than many sparrows. Our country is embroiled in a race war that is unprecedented.

Let me speak briefly about the church. The responsibility of the church is twofold, One, caring for the widows and orphans, or the welfare of people. Along with that the church has a responsibility to act as a foundation for the values of society. The church has abdicated the responsibility of welfare to the government. A responsibility that God never meant for the government to have I would like to speak about the churches responsibility of guarding the biblical values we hold hear.

That is the role the Church is supposed to play in our society and the world.

What does that role of guardian of the biblical values look like? The Bible says that we, as Christians, the church, are to be the salt of the earth, but if the salt has lost its flavor it is only good to be thrown out. The Bible also says in I Peter 4:17"the judgement begins at the house of God"

There has been a lot going on in our country lately. From attacks on our president to a struggle with a worldwide pandemic. Then the rioting going on in our streets in numerous cities across our country. The acceptance of abortion legalized up to the time of birth. The acceptance of transsexual and same sex marriage. I could go on but at the risk of becoming depressed I will refrain. Could it be that the church is responsible for the condition of our country and the world.

I believe that because the church and especially its leaders who have not been preaching and teaching the scriptural values including repentance and leading a Holy Life. That the church has set back and allowed God to be removed from our schools, our government, and our society.

I believe that pastors and all Christians have an obligations to speak out about values that are unbiblical, such as abortion and the homosexual agenda. I am afraid that a lot of pastors are reluctant to speak out on the subjects because of the risk of upsetting some who are sitting in the pews of the church. We are to be biblically correct not socially correct, I am sure that there are some pastors that are afraid of losing their non-profit status because of speaking out on these values. I have always told my employers when I have worked in the secular work force that they are not my source. But that God is my source. I think that the church needs to realize that the government is not their source but that God is their source.

I believe that the disengagement from the culture by Christians has left a void in America that is now being filled by everything anti-Christ and everything the left liberalist can throw at the world.

I am afraid the Sunday-go-to-meeting Christianity will not cut it in our society anymore. I am going to make a prediction here. I predict that if the right person does not get elected in the 2020 election that within 10 years the church will be an under-ground church in America.

I think that some of the problem that the church is struggling with is that issues that are spoken about in scripture, once they become a political issue they refrain from speaking about them. We are to preach scripture at all times not just when it socially accepted. It seems that society has convinced Christians that moral values in the Bible such as life or marriage are no longer the purview of the church once they become political.

I believe that it is no wonder that each generation within the church gets a little less Christian then the following. When we put our kids into an educational system that is skewed to be very anti-America and anti-Bible, the result is what we now see: many Christians apparently believe there is no absolute moral truth. If there is no moral absolutes then how can we teach, especially on one hour on Sunday, that there is any wrong?

Another big problem in the church is just plain apathy. There are very few Evangelical pastors that are actually preach against sin. They like to preach on faith—and there's nothing wrong with that—but many of the sermons just make you feel good when you go home. Having a great church service is fine but today's services rarely mobilize members to change the culture or turn out to vote in crucial elections.

No American church I know of today is being accused of teaching hard stuff and driving people away, with true disciples remaining in the church to be taught more.

And this is part of the problem we face today. As the culture declines and becomes more hostile to Christians and biblical principles, it boils down to a failure of the church in that there's no teaching on holiness that would change people's lives and then motivate them to go out and change the culture

The contemporary, self-effacing church culture hidden behind the walls of the meeting place is not up to Christianity's standards. A different type of church will be required for America to be born again. Budgets, buildings, and bodies in seats can't be the theological focal point if America is to survive. Christians operating in the public square must be empowered by wisdom from above.

Getting the church to be the church is necessary if we are to turn the tide in the culture—and make a difference, because so much is at stake in our culture.

CHURCH WITHOUT GOD IS SIMPLY JUST A GATHERING!

SECTION IV

Government

CHAPTER 9

"There is a rank due to the United States among nations which will be withheld, if not absolutely lost, by the reputations of weakness. If we desire to avoid insult, we must be able to repel it; if we desire to secure peace, one of the most powerful instruments of rising prosperity it must be known that we are at all times ready for war."

President George Washington
Fifth Annual address, December 3, 1793

Your civil liberties mean nothing, if you're dead. That's why the main most important function of the federal government is national defense.

German philosopher George Wilhelm Frederick Hegel describes the state (government) as a body or human being and goes through a growing process.

If we consider the state to be a human being and there is a creator of human beings then it would follow that there is a creator of the state or government.

Hegel also states that there is virtue (values) within the state that all parts of the body must adhere to. Then it follows that there must be an absolute truth that these virtues are based on. When we take away that absolute truth then there is no basis for virtue.

For me, the absolute truth is Jesus and His word (logos). "I am the way, the truth, and the life" Back in the 60's and 70's that absolute truth was taken out of the government (state) in America and thus our virtue was sucked out of our society. The basis for our government lost its truth and foundation

I will go one step further and state that national defense is the federal government's only function. Period. That defense includes protection from all enemies, foreign and domestics. Including in that, Police, sheriffs, and National Guard.

Today, we have things going on around the world, and even here at home that seems like no one respects authority. Police brutality, gun control, the court system, even parents are not allowed to do their God-given jobs. The government has their fingers in every area of our lives.

At the time of the writing of this book, our federal government is in a deplorable shape. Our two-party system is not working except to perpetuate itself. We need to reign in our government back in and move the power back to "the people" where it belongs. Our nation is, in excess, of $20 trillion in debt and it can only get worse.

The only purpose of the government is for protection from any enemies, foreign or domestic, which includes the protection of our freedoms as spelled out in our constitution. It's hard to tell anymore which side is more corrupt, the democrats or republicans. The media has chosen not to report the news but instead to give opinions and allegations as to what is going on each day. They are free to say whatever they want as our constitution gives the press freedom to do that.

I am convinced that our government is not run anymore by people that we have elected but is run entirely by money. Follow the money and you will see why decisions are made in our congress. We can see people get elected to congress rather meeker in their economic status and suddenly they become rich as they are lured in making decisions by those that control the money. Those that are elected to office seem to get rich by bowing to all the interest groups that send their lobbyist to buy votes to keep congress from passing legislation hindering them from doing business to gain them more wealth.

Let me share some thoughts of our condition of America at this moment. We have just endured 8 years of the reign, as President Obama, a progressive, that has taken our country to the brink of disaster.

Most people in the know, know that Obama was a student of Saul Alinsky and his book, "Rules for Radicals". Alinsky put forth the ideology that the ultimate goal is power. Any means of acquiring that power is right and justified.

Practicing deception to conceal one's true goals and regarding moral principles and laws as applicable to others but not to oneself are the core concepts of Alinsky's, "Rules for Radicals". Alinsky's thoughts were that they organize not to help others, as they would have you believe, but for the acquiring of power.

Contrast this ideology with what Christ taught that there is ultimate truth, that His truth" and that the greatest is to be the servant to all". That his truth consist of that real power really comes with serving people. Maybe that is why progressives have no regard for religion because it takes away their idea of power.

The problem is the progressives think they have the truth and if you don't carry the same thirst for power, you have a weak philosophy and different and illegitimate truth.

As of this writing, we are embroiled in a narrative, all over our country, as to whether or not our recent election was filled with fraud. I predict that if we don't get to the truth and that the public can be assured that elections are secure, than this may be the last election we have in America.

The quest for power as the first priority, the need to conceal one's true agenda, and assurance that the rules don't apply to radicals, progressives, who break them in service to the cause, make up the core message of Alinsky's teaching. These are the political guidelines for modern progressives and the Democratic Party today.

I have been working with the Convention of States Initiative organization to try to get the resolution to call for a Convention of States passed in each state. At this point there is no specific agenda for the convention. I think that the convention of states should address two items that will reign in our run-away government back to reality.

1. To pass an amendment to the constitution to put term limits on Congress.
2. Secondly, to make the government to be more fiscal responsible.

We forget, sometimes that the government has no money of their own to spend. It is our money through our tax dollars. As I have stated previously, our indebtedness is over $20 trillion and growing. We will not be able to sustain even paying the interest on our debt soon. Gradually, though no one remembers exactly how it happened, the unthinkable becomes tolerable. And then acceptable. And then legal. And then applaud able."

The government operates like "we the people" gave them our personal credit card and told them to get whatever they think they need to do their job. Would you do that even to a friend and give them no limits. That is insane! The only purpose of the government is for protection of the people and the freedom that the Constitution gives everyone. At this time money runs our government. The power goes to where the money is. Those that are elected to office seem to get rich by bowing to all the interest groups that send their lobbyist to buy votes to keep congress from passing legislation hindering them from doing business honestly or dishonestly.

Most Christians will readily admit that internal transformation comes before the external behavior, but we concentrate on the external because it is most obvious.

The visible, external crises of lost religious freedom, mounting debt, government encroachment cry for attention and are serious problems. But they are just problems that exist because a lack of spiritual influence by the body of Christ in Society, and not making disciples of all nations.

Governments may attempt to aid disadvantaged families and neighborhoods through financial assistance, but positive and permanent change seldom occurs simply by handing out cash. Without the personal touch of people who genuinely care, social welfare usually becomes a wasteful tax burden. But when finances are used to fuel the work of an existing core of concerned people, such as the church, the impact is visible and meaningful. I believe government has a role in our lives, but its role is limited. When the church accepts its God given role in our country, there is no limit to the positive influence it can have on individuals and our country.

We can kiss freedom in America good-bye unless those who say they know, and love God stand together against the forces of evil. I do not want to be found among those who will ask what we were doing when freedom died.

Webster defines the word "politics" as, "the activities, actions and policies that are used to gain and hold power in a government or to influence government; or a person's opinions about the management of government."

Politics can shape the future, but ultimately politics reflect the culture. People of faith can still vote, but we have been culturally limited. Things that were once considered part of our society have been extracted from our society by the government, which has had a devastating effect on our country. Marriage is a church institution, but it has been taken over by the government. Abortion is a moral issue, but it has been politicized. Even welfare and health care were once strongholds of religious responsibility, but now religious organizations are being forced to forsake their convictions or get out of the business of helping others.

There was a situation awhile back, where a baker was asked to prepare a cake for a same sex marriage and the baker refused because it went against his religious beliefs. He was told by the government that he must make the cake or be fined. He decided to close his bakery rather to prostitute his values and make the cake. He ended up winning his court case. If he had refused to make the case on any other grounds he probably would not have had any trouble. The moral climate of our country has put pressure on many of our Christian institutions.

Our compassion in this country has become a take and redistribute instead of individuals voluntarily giving from their abundance. Our leaders have ceased to be leaders and instead protectors of their own turf. I have become a strong advocate of term limits for our congress. Justice in our country has become an arbitrary thing.

America's pharaoh is not a person or a political party. It is a power source other than God upon which people erroneously and foolishly depend—and even begin to worship. The creativity in any one person's mind is enormous.

I am convinced that the two- party system no longer works in America. Both parties are coming to point where they are going two different directions for the good of the party and not America.

The truth is this: When Christian principles are reduced in America, then government grows in size and power.

James Robison in his book "The Steam" makes the following statement:

When God and spiritual life decreases in importance, government expands rapidly. The less we hear God's unadulterated word, the duller our hearing. When the oration loses its conscience, the pulpit is to blame

While everyone may long for freedom at some level, yet people will give up their freedom without a fight if promised security. Many of the government's welfare programs promise financial security but end up causing bondage and loss of freedoms.[5]

Private sector, local community and church programs consistently prove to be more effective in assisting the poor but when government becomes involved in supporting programs that function effectively, one of the first things they do is to demand that references to God be stopped along with faith, prayer, and religious expressions. As a result, government immediately eliminate the main reason the programs are successful.

One of our founding fathers, James Madison said, "In framing a government which is to be administered by men over men, the great an affectivity lies in this; you must first enable the government to control the governed; and in the next place oblige it to control itself.

I am so concerned about our society looking to the federal government to solve our problems. I realize that private citizens too often live irresponsible, out-of-control lives that force the law to step in to protect others and serve justice. But even here the handcuffs and prison bars can only go so far. The Christian witness is what will move people and communities from brokenness to flourishing.

My challenge is for concerned Americans to come together to stop the disaster of mismanaged and overreaching government actions. We need to put the responsibility back in the hands of the families and communities— as we love our God and serve our neighbors.

Daniel Webster has been quoted as saying,

"There is no nation on earth powerful enough to accomplish our overthrow. . . Our destruction, should it come at all, will be from another quarter. From the inattention of the people to the concerns of their government, from their carelessness and negligence. I must confess that I do apprehend some danger. I fear that they may place too implicit confidence in their public servants and fail to properly scrutinize their conduct that in this way they may be made the dupes of designing men and become the instruments of their own undoing".[37]

The question today is not whether we know what's wrong with our country—we see that our government is infringing upon the rights of the populace. Nor is the question whether we have ways to solve the problem. Because of the founder's wisdom, we have all the tools we need to reduce the power of the federal government. We have legislative, judicial, and executive channels for remedying overreach. We have the means to amend the constitution when needed. We have all the legal backup we need to stand up for the rights of the people.

The question is, are we willing to educate ourselves and the courage to stand up to government overreach and use those tools that have been given to us. We must rally a grassroots army to stand up and say, "Enough is enough"

One such movement is the Convention of States Initiative, based on Article V of our constitution which gives the states the power to call a Convention of States, for proposing Amendments to the constitution. Article V states that two-thirds of the states may call a convention of states or, at the moment, 34 states can call for a convention of states. Then three-fourths of the states, or 38 states must pass any amendments that are proposed.

The thoughts that are most prevalent, now, are the fiscal responsibility of the federal government, or the thought to curb the indebtedness of our country. And the term limits of congress and Supreme Court.

One of our biggest problems that we see is the Supreme Court's interpretation of the phrase in our constitution, "general welfare". If a law is just protecting a certain group of people, it cannot be construed to be "general welfare".

The scripture says that we will always have the poor with us. The question is how we as a civilized country based on Christian principles deal with it. We must ask the question, "Is it the responsibility of government to take care of the poor." The answer is, it is not.

I believe the answer lies in the private citizen and the groups that make up our society, such as business, industry, Wall Street, churches and other community groups to step up and be compassionate with those that are struggling.

The problem with government programs are they are often faceless, and unsustainable. I refer back to the illustration of working for the Salvation Army and then with the state DHS agency. The government just keeps printing money to cover its vendors and there are consequences to that kind of actions. Another thing that happens with government programs is that it creates a dependent society. When the majority of the population is relying on government to support them, then there is not enough resources coming in to do the assistance.

Thomas Paine wrote the first of his "American Crises" articles in 1776. Paine's words were written more than 240 years ago but they are just as compelling today as they were then:

> "These are the times that try men's souls. The summer soldier and the sunshine patriot will in this crises, shrink from the service of his country, but he that stands it now, deserves the love and thanks of man and woman. Tyranny, like hell, is not easily conquered; yet we have this consolation with us, that the harder the conflict, the more glorious the triumph. What we obtain too, we esteem to lightly; 'tis dearness only that gives everything its value. Heaven knows how to put a proper price upon goods, and it would be strange indeed, if so celestial an article as freedom should not be highly rated."[6]

GOVERNMENT WITHOUT GOD IS
JUST ORGANIZED CHAOS!

SECTION V

Steps Back to Freedom

CHAPTER 10

Now comes the hard part. After discussing the problems and some of the reasons that got us to this point, I am going to try to give some solutions. Some will take years to solve, if not generations. It is going to involve a complete mindset change for all of society in America and the world for that matter.

I am worried about our country and the direction it appears to be going. Mostly I worry about the generations that are already born and taking on a different morality and sense of spiritual deadness.

WE need in this generation or the next need to take our message rightness and morality to every nook and cranny of our society. Into not only our church buildings, but into the family dinner table, to the court rooms, the schools, the work place and in every legislature across our land. We must be the leaven that changes the whole society

Actually, we don't have to go clear back to the sixties for an example. As I am writing this, we are in the midst of protests and rioting about the death of African American man at the hands of police. The rioters are burning down public buildings like court houses and destroying people businesses and taking down statues of important people in the history of our country. I believe there has to be someone or some organization that are convincing people to do this to further some political cause.

I am going to try and tackle each area separately, and then collectively. Fixing the Family unit is key to the change overall. Once we solve the broken family problem, much of what we are dealing with in the other areas will ultimately fix themselves.

It's easy to point out the problems in our society and even complain about them, but it's another thing to take action in pursuit of the way you think they should be.

I believe that there are several things that need to happen in order to save our country. Our total philosophical thinking process needs to be centered in the Constitution and to the adherents that are brought forth in it.

A free country will never remain free if it does not have a center for truth to have at its foundation. For our American society, that truth must be based upon our Creator, in whom all things derive their being. God created society not that society has created a God and precepts to live by.

Once we move more to the center of our founding fathers intentions within the Constitution, we will reverse directions and begin a journey back to the country our founding fathers intended.

I think the only way our country will be fixed is for the church to stand up and be counted. And the first step in doing that is to be on our knees in prayer. As it says in II Chronicles 7:14,

> Then if my people who are called by my name will humble themselves and pray and seek my face and turn from their wicked ways, I will hear from heaven and will forgive their sins and restore their land. My eyes will be open and my ears attentive to every prayer made in this place. For I have chosen this Temple and set it apart to be holy—a place where my name will be honored forever. I will always watch over it, for it is dear to my heart.

At the start of the Constitutional Convention, the framers of our country decided that the law should be supreme, (i.e. the Constitution) but in these modern days we have made man, the populace the supreme thing.

Thus, the law Changes with every whim of the populace. In the beginning of our nation, the framers of the Constitution set the work of our government with our congress making the law in the legislative branch, the Executive branch enforcing the law and the Judicial branch keeping the law within the framework of the Constitution.

Let me put out three statements of fixing the four institutions that God has ordained for our nation, which in turn will fix our government. I will enlarge on these statements in the last chapters of this book.

I)   To provide a privatization of our educational system across the country. Take education back to communities by giving back to counties. Take the funding out of federal government hands and place in counties. Institute County boards to make local decisions in education. These boards made up of parents who will decide the direction each school district will go with education. Remove the thought that parents are not qualified to educate their children. Perhaps a home owners association fee or use property taxes to fund.

We must try to turn the "me" generation into the "them" generation and raise up a servant mentality.

II) Mobilize the church community

1.   Encourage an organizational structure to put in place helps for the community (a welfare system in the private sector). The scripture says in Matthew that as Christians we are to be the light of the world. Our light is to shine into the darkness of this world. We are also are told that we are the salt of the earth. Salt is a substance that changes the flavor of whatever it is applied to. I am afraid that Christians (the church) has for too long kept its salt in the salt shaker as within the four walls of church buildings. I, with a heart problem, am on a low sodium diet. Perhaps the church has been on a low sodium diet for too long and have lost our saltiness. We are not being the light in the world that it needs, and neither are we allowing the salt to change the flavor of our country or the world.

III) To put in place a political community to elect pro-private, value candidates.

To support a Convention of states initiative to put the power and authority back in the local community hands. One of the biggest problems we have in our government is that our congressmen have been in office to long. Our founders never meant to have professional politicians but community servants.

If we help change the political philosophy through the church and Christian people speaking up and taking an active part in the change, we have already begun to change the way we govern in America.

In Proverbs 28:2, King Solomon says, "When there is moral rot within a nation, its government topples easily. But wise and knowledgeable leaders bring stability"

We have much moral rot in our country. For a country that was founded upon Christian principles to be in such moral decay means that our country will be easily toppled either by foreign powers or from within.

Many of our presidents have spoken in speeches and mentioned the biblical phrase that America is, "a city set on a Hill" shining its light throughout the world. Even President Obama eluded that we are a nation of many religions, Christianity, Muslim and others. George Washington in his address to the nation mentions, "The Almighty Being who rules over the universe".

A couple of decades before Obama's declaration about our religious diversity, a soon to be president made another reference to our religious culture. Less than two weeks before intoning "ask not what your country can do for you" during his own inaugural address in 1961, John F. Kennedy reminded the legislature in his home state, of John Winthrop's words:

> I have been guided by the standard John Winthrop set before his shipmates on the flagship 'Arabella' three hundred and thirty-one years ago, as they, too, faced the task of building a new government on a perilous frontier. 'We must consider, he said, 'that we shall be as a city upon a hill—the eyes of all people are upon us.' Today the eyes of all people are truly upon us—and our governments, in every branch, at every level, national, state and local, must be as a city upon a hill—constructed and inhabited by men aware of their great trust and their great responsibilities. For we are setting out upon a voyage in 1961 no less hazardous than that undertaken by the 'Arabella' in 1630. We are comps of statecraft no less fantastic than that of

governing the Massachusetts Bay Colony, beset as it was then by terror without and disorder within.[7]

In 1974, Ronald Reagan offered his own religious interpretation of this early moment in American history:

"… Some divine plan that placed this great continent between two oceans to be sought out by those who were possessed of an abiding love of freedom and a special kind of courage. This was true of those who pioneered the great wilderness in the beginning of this country, as it is also true of those later immigrants who were willing to leave the land of their birth and come to a land where even the language was unknown to them, call it chauvinistic, but our heritage does set us apart."

President Ronal Reagan upon leaving office in January 1989, referenced his vision of what "city on a hill" might look like in his speech, when he said:

"The past few days when I've been at that window upstairs, I've thought a bit of the "shining city upon a hill," The phrase comes from John Winthrop, who wrote it to describe the America he imagined. What he imagined was important because he was an early Pilgrim, an early freedom man. He journeyed here on what today we'd call a little wooden boat; and like the other Pilgrims, he was looking for a home that would be free.

I've spoken of the shining city all my political life, but I don't know if I ever quite communicated what I saw when I said it. But in my mind, it was a tall, proud city built on rocks stronger than oceans, wind-swept, God-blessed, and teeming with people of all kinds living in harmony and peace; a city with free ports that hummed with commerce and creativity. And if there had to be city walls, the walls had doors and the doors were open to anyone with the will and the heart to get here. That's how I saw it and see it still.

And how stands the city on this winter night? More prosperous, more secure and happier than it was 8 years ago. But more than that: After 200 years, two centuries, she still stands strong and true on the granite ridge, and her glow has held steady no matter what storm. And she's still a beacon, still a magnet for all who must have freedom, for all the pilgrims from all the lost places who are hurtling through the darkness toward home.

CHAPTER 11

Fixing The Family

A statement that we hear often is "you cannot legislate morality." I totally agree with that statement. If that was not true, once we make a law, everyone would abide by it and we know that this is so not true.

Studies have shown that once a mother and father divorce, the children, no matter how they try and think about divorce, they are more likely to be divorced in their adult relationship. So how do we fix the problem of divorce? Several things come to mind. One, make it harder to get divorced and harder to marry. Counseling should be required in both cases.

The family is a link in the church chain and the stronger each link is the stronger the church is. The reverse is also true. The weaker the link is the weaker the church is and weaker the influence the church is on society.

The family is the foundation of the church. In fact, God speaks in His word, that the church is the bride of Christ. He talks about the marriage between the two and how the groom, Christ, presents the bride, the church, as spotless. This gives us a design for what an earthly marriage is to be like.

The family unit is the stronghold of a nation. Once you have destroyed the family unit, you will begin to dismantle and destroy a nation or community.

When the Israelites left Jerusalem and went into captivity in Egypt their home country and city had been destroyed. So, when they returned to Jerusalem and their home country and city laid in ruins, they began to gather together to rebuild, beginning with the wall around the city. They first began to rebuild the wall of protection around the physical city. Nehemiah, their leader, called the people together, and set them in family units to stand in the gaps and to begin rebuilding the wall in front of their home' He set up the rebuilding process with family units. The family is the most important part of a nation and community. Nehemiah knew that the family unit was the key to bringing the nation back from destruction.

The family is not only the foundation of the church but the foundation for government and society.

America has had the blessings of God throughout its history. The nation of Israel is said to be God's chosen people. God has blessed the Nation of Israel throughout its history but when it has strayed from the commandments of God, it has lost the blessings throughout its history, including bondage to another nation. Prolonging America's days of blessings only freedom makes possible, depends on the response of God's church to the demands being made today by those who reject the truth as revealed by nature's God and nature's law. The church of Jesus Christ will either take a stand on God's irrefutable truth or we will witness the fall of our once-great nation.

I am not sure that any of the four institutions can be fixed separately. The main problem is that we have gone astray of our Christian moral value systems that our forefathers had when they founded this great nation.

It is disturbing when I realize that the divorce rate in the church is just as large as the secular world. We have always taught in the church that putting Christ as the center of the home will build strong marriages and families. I think the problem has been that we don't understand what putting Christ at the center of the home really means. Having believing parents is not the only thing that needs to happen. Parents need to understand that it doesn't come automatically when both parents are believers. It has to be intentional. It means that the parents have a daily quiet time and pray every day for their own guidance and for their children to be protected from the enemy's cunning schemes. It means that the family prays together and not just at meals. It means the family studies God's word faithfully. I am sure that many people are thinking when is there time to do all this when we have work, household duties, school, sports activities etc. We have time to do the important things. What do you consider important?

The scripture says, "You shall know the truth and the truth will make you free." I believe that the truth that the scripture speaks of is the invaluable word of God. In that word of God, it is presented as truth is embodied in the person of Jesus Christ. He declared himself to be "the truth, and the life" No man comes to the father except through me." Until we as a country come back to that truth, true freedom will be elusive at best, and nonexistent at worst. God, "logos" "the word" is the truth. "Logos" is the same person of truth that was existent at the time of creation when it is said, "And God "said" (word or logos) let there be light."

It has been said that you cannot legislate morality and I believe, for the most part that is true. I also believe that if we would have stricter laws on marriage and divorce, it might help to stave the divorce rate in our country. If the moral fabric of our country does not change then the laws don't matter. We would just have more couples living together without the commitment of a marriage covenant.

My first wife and I met one day at a local restaurant to divide our material possessions and discussed our future together. I asked her if she was going to file for divorce. She said "No". She had grown up in the church, as I had, and had been taught that divorce was wrong. I am sure that was running through her mind at the time.

I asked her, "Do you think that God is looking down at the court house to see if there was a paper filed, or if He was looking at your heart." I added, "I know in your heart you have already come to the feelings of divorce, so why don't you go ahead and file so that I can get on with my life."

After several months and long discussions, we filed jointly, and I moved to another city and eventually remarried. During that year we were separated, I received counseling to keep my sanity.

I often look back over that time and notice two things. One, I see the footprints of God all over my story. And, two, Only by His Grace that I sit here telling this story in His strength and for His glory.

The family is being hit hard with Satan's attacks. Between skyrocketing divorce ratings, abortion accepted up to the third trimester or even at birth, to open marriage, couples living together, and the acceptance of same sex marriage. The redeeming of the marriage covenant and rebuilding of family units almost seems impossible. We have a great and powerful God and according to His word in John 16:33:

> I have told you all this so that you may have peace in me.
> Here on earth you will have many trials and sorrows. But
> take heart, because I have overcome the world.

CHAPTER 12

Fixing Education

Basically, I see five problems to be fixed in public education.

1) Certification process for teachers
2) Learning methods standardized
3) Technology disadvantages and advantages
4) Discipline methods ineffective
5) Testing and evaluation not effective.

I see that the major problem with our education system is the process of certification. The same broken system has produced the people that are doing the certificating. The question that needs answering is, "What makes a person an expert on a given topic?"

We have been so enamored with our leaders, especially our politicians who parade around as our leaders. Many of those so called leaders who claim to be experts in law and other things that have been in positions of leadership in our country for 30-40 years and we are no more better off than when they started their so called leadership. They claim to be leaders and make laws that are to make us better off but like the examples that began this book do us more harm than good.

Certification:

One way to fix the certification process is to put it back into the local community. Only those in the community will recognize when someone has a gift to teach and the knowledge of each subject.

One of the biggest problems we have today in America with Education is teacher tenure that has been negotiated by the teacher's associations or unions.

This prevents school districts from getting rid of bad teachers and keeping good gifted teachers who have been teaching for shorter periods of time. As I have stated previously, you cannot collectively bargain for something that cannot be standardized. Like Doctors, teachers, cannot be collectively grouped together to standardize a bargaining agreement. Teacher associations should not be used to be unions but professional improvement organizations.

As was stated earlier, certification is the act of a superior entity saying that a lower entity meets certain criteria that gives the lower entity respectability. Maybe we need to start at the top and see what we can ascertain that makes them the superior.

Standardized Testing

We are training teachers to teach to test instead of teaching for knowledge and the needs of preparing students to thrive in the world after schooling. One of the problems with standardized testing is that the standards keep changing. Students either know the subject or they don't. We cannot keep lowering the standard so that the test scores improve. We need to make sure that the students are learning the material for creating a life, not to take a test. Then the test scores will take care of themselves.

It was not until I was in college that I learned how to take test. A biology professor finally taught me how to learn a set of materials. Instead of learning a rote set of muscles or bones, he asked questions like, "When you are doing sit-ups, what muscle groups are you using?" He taught for life, not to take a test.

Technology-good or bad

Technology in the classroom can be a great tool for teaching. The problem with technology is that it really brings students a method of socializing and not a method of learning.

Why do you need to learn anything and stash it into your brain when you can get any information you desire with a push of a button with your finger and it quickly appears on a small screen? Maybe student's brains are wired differently than older people, but they will lack, for the most part, problem solving skills that will be required later in life.

Once when I was substitute teaching, I happen to have lunch room duty. My assignment was to walk around the lunch room and keep the students from being too rowdy and to make sure they cleaned up their tables. As I was walking around the room, I noticed a guy and a girl sitting across the table from each other and they were face timing each other. I thought at the time, "Is this what the world is coming to when it comes to socializing. We have to be looking at a screen instead of into the person's eyes and communicating emotions and thoughts. A screen is so impersonal and words on a screen do not express the expressions on a face and tone of voice. In some ways, technology has brought us one step forward and two steps back.

I heard that there are school districts that were using I-pads or Laptops for textbooks for several years. They realized that text scores were falling each year. They have returned to hard cover text books and found out that text scores began to improve. They found out that students seemed to retain more by reading a paper page and turning pages in textbooks than on a screen. They also realized that with I-pads students could look busy on the I-pads but actually doing something besides the assigned lesson. They also found out that students actually preferred the hard copies. I would assume that there were less distractions with the hard copy than the I-pads. It might even help their physical development with a hard copy as the weight in carrying them around all day and back and forth to home puts activity with muscular development

During the pandemic of 2020, many schools closed and went to online learning. Many students are falling behind because of lack of physical contact with caring teachers. Unless there is monitoring at home to keep them on task, they are not getting the help and tutoring that is necessary for complete learning.

A University of Maryland study in 2017 found there was little difference in the two formats when students were asked about the general themes of a text, but the printed version made them better able to answer specific questions.

The study's authors suggested print be preferred when an assignment demands more engagement or deeper comprehension, or if students—primary, secondary or tertiary—were required to read more than one page or 500 words.

As for the weight of the textbooks in backpacks, Mr. Pitcairn said students could leave them in their lockers or use a digital version at home. "I've noticed that students prefer their textbook in both places," he said.

Perhaps we have jumped on the technological bandwagon too quickly. At least it deserves a second look as to whether it is a help or hindrance

Discipline Methods

Once again, the government has over regulated so that the schools cannot appropriately discipline a student. A teacher cannot use any kind of physical restraint on a student or they will have a lawsuit on their hands. The government has taken away the right to have corporal punishment in the classroom. The only leverage the teacher has is to sentence the student to in school suspension or send the student to a principle or counselor. The principle or counselor's only leverage is to suspend the student. Which is probably what the student wants in the first place. They have no desire to learn and so they do not want to be in that environment.

As was stated before, the worst thing that has happened to our education system is the rule of mandatory education. They have to be there. When there is competition between students, parents, schools and communities, there will be better outcomes. I realize that this is a slippery slope to be going down. We do have freedom to get an education, but it is a privilege and not an entitlement.

We read in Proverbs 12:1

To learn you must love discipline.

It is stupid to hate correction.

This is so true, and I believe our public schools have forgotten this truth and allowed our students to do what they think best instead of using discipline to correct their bad behavior.

CHAPTER 13

Fixing The Church

Christ said about the church, "Upon this rock I will build my church, and the gates of hell will not prevail against it."

I am not sure that the "real Church" needs fixing as the scripture says above. However, I truly believe that if the church begins to operate on Biblical ideas and truths that it can be the answer to fixing the problems of family and government in our country and in the world.

My question has been for many years that the church believed for many years that it was not its job to get involved in government or politics, so it allowed the culture to be influenced by the enemy and thus pulled the culture father away from biblical principles. Case in point, when Madalyn Murry O'Hare got prayer and the bible banned from our public schools. Also, we, as the church, have allowed the killing of thousands of unborn children through abortion practices around the country. We have allowed law makers to make laws that are not based on the principles that our founding fathers held dear when establishing this great nation.

I am afraid that for years, the organized church (religion) has done more damage than good.

A Christian is a person who, with all the honesty of which he is capable becomes convinced that the fact of Jesus Christ is the most trustworthy that he knows in his entire universe of language. Christ thus becomes both his central postulate and the fulcrum which because it is really firm, enables him to operate with confidence in other areas.

A lack of church programs and entertainment is not why our youth are leaving the church. Our youth have no relationship with Jesus and that begins at home. Until we focus on fixing that, all the entertainment in the world won't keep them.

I believe that the reason that church plants are becoming the growth of the church is because they are emphasizing relational ministry and not program type ministry. There is also one problem with most church plants is that the theology is very shallow. Relationships mean a lot to everyone. Staring into a screen is not an effective relational atmosphere. The church needs to become relational in all areas of the common person's life (i.e. social, educational, political, and Spiritual).

As I was scrolling through Facebook the other day, I came across a comment by Franklin Graham, who is the leader of the Billy Graham Evangelistic Association. He was endorsing Donald Trump as a presidential candidate for a second term. It is my understanding that any non-profit organization who promotes a political candidate would lose their non-profit status. At least this is the biggest reason that churches use to not be involved with the political process, thus their constituents would not cannot be able to use their donations as a tax deduction.

A quote from "Kingdom Warriors of God" says this, "We will never change the world by going to church. We will only change the World by being the church."

I really believe Christ's words spoken in Matthew 5:13-16,

> "You are the salt of the earth. But what good is salt if it has lost its flavor? Can you make it salty again? It will be thrown out and trampled underfoot as worthless.
>
> You are the light of the world—like a city on a hilltop that cannot be hidden. No one lights a lamp and then puts it under a basket. Instead, a lamp is placed on a stand, where it gives light to everyone in the house. In the same way, let your good deeds shine out for all to see, so that everyone will praise your heavenly Father."

We do not get involved with community to bring them to church, but to influence society and bring Christ's kingdom into hearts of people and to bring Biblical values to the forefront. People do not have to be brought to a building to receive a relationship with Christ. I have always said that many time to people that your actions are so loud that I can't hear what you are saying.

I believe there are two ways that we are going to have to address, in order to fix the church.

1. Get outside of the church walls. We have become brick and mortar oriented rather than people oriented. We must become involved with our community and its needs both physical and spiritual. We must become the vehicle to address the social concerns of our society.

2. We must become the voice of God in our society. We must become part of the political process. I truly believe that our country is based on the laws of the Bible, (i.e. the Ten Commandments). As such, the church needs to continually be a part of the law-making process and not leave it up to our politicians who may or may not ascribe to the scriptural foundation of this country.

3. We must become aggressively evangelistic. We should love people into the kingdom. Also, there are too many Christians still chained to addiction including some of our leaders in our churches.

As I have studied God's word, I have come across the concept of "Logos" the Greek word for "Word" or "speak". We find this concept throughout scripture. In Genesis, we read "In the beginning" and "God spoke and it was". The concept of "Logos". God's voice, or just his "being" and it created the world. It's the same concept in the written word. The scripture in the written form in the black and white. In the first chapter of the Gospel of John we read:

> "In the beginning the Word already existed, The word was with God and the Word was God. He existed in the beginning with God. God created everything through him, and nothing was created except through him.

The Word gave life to everything that was created, and his life brought light to everyone. The light shines in the darkness, and the darkness can never extinguish it."

Many times as I have preached to my congregation, there have been people who have come to me after the service and ask me the question, "Have you been secretly hiding at our house this week because your message was like you have been there and were aware of everything that has gone on at home?" Always, my answer was, "No, but the Word, (logos) was, because it is alive and active" God's spirit is hovering around our existence.

In Matthew 6, we read what is commonly called the Lord's Prayer. Actually it should be called, "The Disciples Prayer" as he was teaching the disciples how to pray. One of the phrases he uses in the prayer that we are supposed to pray is, "May your will be done on earth, as it is in heaven."

I don't think that we really realize what that phrase means. God does not want our world to be what it has become. I think that we as Christians are supposed to look forward to heaven when we can enjoy all the good things that God has prepared for us. God wants us to enjoy the good things of heaven here on this earth. Not only are we to pray for that to happen, we are to be the salt of the earth, and the light of the world and make it happen.

When we sit back as Christians, and let the light go out in our country, we are not being the light that will not let the darkness overwhelm it. It is time for Christians to stand up and be counted on to not just pray that the light will shine in the darkness but to be the light especially in our government and in the political arena. I am afraid that if we do not, that we have reached a juncture in our history that we will no longer be able to call ourselves a Christian nation.

I think, historically, the church tends to take the greatest promises of Scripture and put them off into a period of time for which we have no responsibility. Jesus commanded His followers to do things that they might have impact now. His assignment to His followers was always to bring transformation to their immediate surroundings. In the prayer that Christ gives to us in Matthew, chapter 6, we see the importance the Father gives to being concerned about our world today. He invites us into interaction with our world that we know, to be co-laboring to be light and transform our world from darkness to His light.

God wants His world, Heaven, to have overriding influence on this one that we live in, in the here and now. As Christians, we need to be agents in changing our culture. Fist we need to understand our culture and what or how it is now and how do we influence it for the better.

Not too long ago, I watched a video of a speaker who was trying to explain how a man and woman's brain works differently. He said that a man takes every subject and puts it in little boxes and files it away and only pulls the box out for that subject when he needs it. The woman's brain is all connected to each other and can be talking about several things at once and everything is connected to everything else. I think the church tends to operate in a similar fashion to man's brain. We have a box for every part of our lives and only pull it out when we need it. Christians tend to compartmentalize Christianity and only pull it out when we need it. We almost keep our Christianity inside the four walls of the church and pull it out when we are in church. The world then tends to influence the church instead of vice versa. We need to change that structure of the church.

Culture is basically the values, principles, beliefs, and attitudes that influence how life is lived in a specific location. Every local group of people, as in a city and nation or church. The goal is to taste and see what it would be like to have "Heaven's" culture shape the value system of the world we live in.

Heaven' culture is actually the ever-presence of God. That is the focus of the culture of Heaven. Everything in Heaven is connected to and thrives because of the presence of God. There is nothing in Heaven that exists apart from His presence. The culture of Heaven is the beauty of that surrounds His presence.

I say all that, to say this: The church has not influenced our world to become a Heavenly culture. The question that we need to answer is, when the church is going to begin to stand up for the values of scripture with no regard for being politically correct or the consequences of taking stands that seem to be unpopular in the culture we live in. We have allowed the liberal values to dictate our nation's culture, when the body of Christ, the church needs to be dictating the values of heaven here on earth and our nation.

Mark Shaner, a member of one of the first teams that went to Russia to spread the gospel to the Russian people visited a store in a suburban neighborhood in the city of Chelyabinsk, in Siberia. Upon leaving the store, his group of American visitors noticed the bare shelfs in the store. Mark shares in his book, "To Russia With God's Love" this experience by sharing the conversation he had with their Russian counterparts in Education.

> Back on the bus, I asked Albert Akmalov, a literature teacher at Lyceum #31, "How long has it been like this?" I expected an answer something like, "Since last October, when the prices soared. But understand, this is not indicative of the entire country."

> But instead Albert said, "It's been like this since the Revolution of 1917. Statisticians predict that, before the end of this year there will be mass Starvation."

> I was quiet as I pondered this possibility. Then Albert added quietly, "The only thing that will change Russia is if we let God back into our country."[8]

This story from Mark's visit to Russia sounds very sad as he shares from a very emotional experience. But I am afraid that America is on the brink of this same scenario if the church does not wake up and stand up for their Christian values and be the "Logos" in society.

CHAPTER 14

Fixing Government

Daniel Webster in one of his publications said this,

> There is no nation on earth powerful enough to accomplish our destruction, should it come at all, will be from another quarter. From the intention of the people to the concerns of their government, from their carelessness and neglect. I must confess that I do apprehend some danger. I fear that they may place to imperfect confidence in their public servants and fail to properly scrutinize their conduct that is this way they maybe made the dupes of designing men and become the instruments of their own undoing.[9]

This was written 61 years after the signing of the Declaration of Independence but is still applicable today.

I have always heard that we have two choices. Two paths to take and one is easy, and its only reward is that it is easy.

I remember hearing President John Kennedy's speech during the space race between the USA and Russia. He said, "We choose to go to space in this decade not because it is easy, but because it is hard."

Some people might think that our government is to far down the road to ruin to fix. As of this writing, I don't think so, but if we do not begin to act now, we might possibly get to that precipice pretty quickly.

One of the biggest problems with government, especially for Christians, is that it has become a god. In other words, instead of looking to God,

Yahweh, as our source for all of our needs, we have looked to the government to take care of us. The result of this is that we become dependent upon government to take care of us. We forget that the government has no resources except what they take from someone else. God is the creator of all things and has everything at His disposal to meet our needs. When I was employed somewhere on a job and was responsible to someone, i.e. a boss, I always made sure they understood that they were not my source and they should not consider it their responsibility to make sure I was taken care of. I tried to work hard, "as unto the Lord" but they were not my source for sustenance.

If the government would concentrate on protection of our country, both foreign and domestic, including military and police in each city across our country, that would be enough for the government and would decrease our tax burden.

German philosopher, George Wilhelm Frederick Hegel, describes the state, (government) as a body or human being and goes through a process.[47]

If we consider the state to be a human being and there is a creator of human being then it would follow that there is a creator of the state (government)

Hegel also states that there is virtue (values) within the state that all parts of the body must adhere to then it follows that there must be an absolute truth that these virtues are based on. When we take away that absolute truth, then there is no basis for virtue.

For me, that absolute truth is Jesus and His word, (logos). "I am the way, the truth and life." Back in the 60's and 70's that absolute truth was taken out of government (state) in America and thus our virtue was sucked out of our society

I am afraid that for centuries we have relied on government to solve our problems in our society. I will go on record to say that government will never solve our problems. Only a right relationship with God, our creator, will solve our problems. I am afraid that the church has not given us a very good representation of our God or what he meant for His church to be.

The way to fix government is to, through the involvement of the average citizen like you and me. We must put the power back into local individuals instead of big government,

I believe the only way of doing this is through a Convention of States.

This means that 34 states must, through their state legislature call for a convention of states for the same purpose. Then according to the United States Constitution Congress must call a convention of states. The place and time will be determined by congress. When this convention convenes, then the delegates, one from each state may move the convention to any place they so desire. When the convention decides on an amendment to the constitution, it must be ratified by three fourths of the states or at the moment 38 states. The most talked about amendments that should be debated at the convention will be 1), term limits for congress and the Supreme Court. And 2) fiscal responsibility in raising taxes and spending limits which could be in the form of a balanced budget.

Another topic that I believe needs to be addressed is protected borders, especially on our southern borders. The progressives in our country are pushing for open borders for two reasons, 1) most of those crossing our borders illegally will vote democratic so it gives them a more powerful base, and 2) it moves the world closer to a one world government. Which in turn will swallow up our freedoms under our constitution.

At the beginning of our country, the Constitutional Convention, the framers of our country decided that the law should be supreme, i.e. the constitution should be supreme but in these modern days we have made man, the populace the supreme thing.

Thus, the law changes with every whim of the populace. In the beginning of our nation the framers of the Constitution set the frame work of government making the law in the legislative branch, the Executive branch enforcing the law and the Judicial branch keeping the law within the framework of the Constitution.

If we ourselves can define what truth is and what it isn't then we are the masters of the universe. If we are the ones to decide what is right and what is wrong then truth becomes our toy and not anything to base our lives on. I think our modern society would call this being politically correct. I think that is why many people in America hate our President Trump as he has never been politically correct. He tells it the way he sees it.

The question becomes, "Who has the power?" Jesus taught that he went to the cross because we did NOT deserve it, not that we deserved it. The reason that Jesus became the enemy of the people was because He challenged the ones that thought they had the power. When they saw their power slowly slipping away, they took things into their own hands and crucified Him.

I am afraid that this is happening today. We are drowning in the moral decay around us. I am not talking about, drugs, crime, abortion or really any action that we have allowed to happen. I am talking about the decay that comes about when there is no "true" truth and the crumbling starts.

I am afraid that we have become self-obsessed and will do anything to keep that train rolling down the tracks.

Those politicians in power at the moment exemplify his statement. Truth as we used to know it that is based on the truth of God's word is no longer relevant.

Jesus taught that Truth is really God's instruction book as to how we are to live our lives and get the satisfaction that we are okay. The problem is that the world thinks this is too confining. Jesus says that this is the only way to true freedom.

You see, the truth that Jesus taught is that man's joy and satisfaction in life is best understood in terms of the spiritual part of man. Being spiritually blind is really what keeps us enslaved.

It has become a battle between two religions. The religion of Humanism, which makes God's of everyone, and Christianity, which looks at the one true God, as the ultimate truth.

Because of some Muslim demanding that states or the Federal government to establish Sharia law is without question unconstitutional because the first amendment guarantees that we will not establish a state or national religion and Sharia law is based on the Muslin religion; it would never be instituted in a country that is based on citizens having freedom to worship who or what they wish. Instituting Sharia law would mean we adhere to the Muslim religion.

GOVERNMENT WITHOUT GOD IS TYRANNY

CHAPTER 15

Conclusion

When I started writing this book, I thought that I could give a solution to each Institution that God has created, at least for our nation. I now have realized that the solution must come collectively, as they are each intertwined with each other.

I thought that I could offer three or four bullet points for each institution to correct the direction our country is going. I now realize that life is not really like that unless you are OCD. I think now it is going to take a nation of Christians to fall on their knees and pray for forgiveness, and that He would place in our hearts the fortitude and strength to stand up for the truth. To become the voice that has not been heard for the last three or four decades. Yes, morality cannot be legislated, but it can be returned by a God-fearing society.

Our government has become so powerful that it cannot be what it needs to be. I think when our country first started our citizens wanted to make our nation a great nation, which we have done. Now, our citizenship has become so proud that we have lost all sight of how we got here. I believe that the overall solution to our country's problems is to return to the humility that got us here in the first place.

Our nation's leaders have become so hungry for power that they will cross any moral line to achieve it. Every person that becomes any kind of leader in our nation's capital, becomes powerful and corrupt.

Our nation was founded on the principles set forth in God's Holy Scripture. God, all through the Old Testament and New Testament emphasized the idea that if you want to be great than you must first humble yourself.

When I have turned their hostility back on them and brought them to the land of their enemies, then at last their stubborn hearts will be humbled, and they will pay for their sins

Leviticus 26:41

Now Moses was very humble—more humble than any other person on earth

Numbers 12:3

You rescue the humble, but your eyes watch the proud and humiliate them.

II Samuel 22:28

You were sorry and humbled yourself before the Lord when you heard what I said against this city and its people—that this land would be cursed and become desolate. You tore your clothing in despair and wept before me in repentance. And I have indeed heard you, says the Lord.

II Kings 22:19

Then if my people who are called by my name will humble themselves and pray and seek my face and turn from their wicked ways, I will hear from heaven and will forgive their sins and restore their land.

II Chronicles 7:14

You rescue the humble, but you humiliate the proud.

Psalm 18:27

He leads the humble in doing right, teaching them his way.

Psalm 25:9

The humble will see their God at work and be glad. Let all who seek God's help be encouraged.

Psalm 69:32

The Lord supports the humble, but he brings the wicked down into the dust

Psalm 147:6

Though the Lord is great, he cares for the humble, but he keeps his distance from the proud.

Psalm 138:6

Human pride will be brought down, and human arrogance will be humbled. Only the Lord will be exalted on that day of judgement.

Isaiah 2:11

God blesses those who are humble, for they will inherit the whole earth.

Matt. 5:5

But those who exalt themselves will be humbled, and those who humble themselves will be exalted.

Matt.23:12

Humble yourselves before the Lord, and he will lift you up in honor.
James 4:10

I have always been intrigued by Bible prophecy and the end of times, as a lot of people are. We want to know what our future holds. We want to know what the future holds for our country. The fascinating thing for me, when I start studying the end times, is that there is no mention of any kind of country from the west being involved in the last battles or anything connected to the end of time, This leads me to believe that America, as we know it, does not exist, or at least is not a world power. That thought should scare us a lot.

I want America to be a shining light into the world as to our belief in the one true God and that He blesses those that follow Him. Unless we come to our senses and change our nation and come back to the principles we were founded on, then we cannot expect to be that shining light to the world.

A few years ago, a church in Georgia released through a subsidiary a film entitled, "The War Room". The opening scene is an actual war room where military generals are devising a strategy to go into battle. The real story in the movie is an elderly lady who goes into her "War Room" for prayer. Through prayer she saves a marriage of a young real estate agent who she met when she was trying to sell her home. She went to battle for this young couple in her prayer room and God began to work on both the husband and wife and saves their marriage.

I am convinced, this may be the only way that our nation, The United States of America can be saved. We need top Christian leaders, Generals, to begin to bring the troops together in battle. To join together as a body of believers to go against the enemy of the souls of men and women, to draw the nation back to God and the moral basis upon which this great country was founded upon. The power of prayer is more powerful than any politician, any philosophical mind set or any weapon of the enemy.

> Then if my people who are called by my name will humble themselves and pray and seek my face and turn from their wicked ways, I will hear from heaven and will forgive their sins and restore their land.

II Chronicles 7:14

The great theologian, Pascal, said this, which solidifies what I have been trying to say:

The Christian religion teaches men these two truths: that there is a God whom men can know, and that there is a corruption in their nature which renders them unworthy of Him. It is equally important to men to know both these points; and it is dangerous for man to know God without knowing his own wretchedness, and to know his own wretchedness, without knowing the Redeemer who can free him from it.

If, with Pascal, we can know and appreciate these two truths we still have a long way to go, but we are certainly on the road. We still have many problems to solve, but we are at least saved from both meaninglessness and pride. Through making use of the fulcrum come burdens are already lifted.

Truth by its very definition is a narrow road. Our modern society has made it a wide path as they proclaim there are no absolutes.

We are being drowned in the flood of moral decay, and I am not talking about sex, drugs or the legalizing of marijuana. I am talking about the decay that comes as result of deciding there's no longer absolute truth. We see it first in our families, removing the sacredness of the marriage vow, to removing the responsibility of educating children from parents. Next it moves to corporate ethics. That is why we see an increase in hate crimes and white-collar crimes and no respect for authorities.

Jesus stepped into a similar environment. He spoke of losing your life on behalf of others in order to save it.

So, I caution our political leaders, to be careful that you don't create a monster that turns on you.

To me, truth is not relative. God's word is non-negotiable. As humans, we tend to take his word that we agree with and live accordingly. If to abide by all His word-ultimate truth, even when it goes against our earthly pleasures does not bring true freedom.

God has set in motion principles for the maximum efficiency and as existence of His creation to ultimately reflect His Glory. God created earth and man for a distinct purpose: to exhibit His creation and glory.

If by writing this book, I have only raised awareness for myself or sold so many books that I become well known, then I have failed. But if I can raise the level of awareness that it develops a change in directions but I am not well known or only sell a few books, then I have been successful in the writing of this book.

As a pastor or a leader in the church we need to remember that "The Truth" is God's playbook. Just as a coach of a sports team must have a play book that gives instructions to each player as to what the coach wants him or her to do.

We find this stated to us within the instruction book that God has given to us. Listen as the apostle Paul tells us in II Timothy 3:16-17:

> "All Scripture is inspired by God and is useful to teach us what is true and to make us realize what is wrong in our lives. It corrects us when we are wrong and teaches us to do what is right. God uses it to prepare and equip his people to do every good work."

True freedom in America is living in God's truth even in the area of government. We do not want or need a national religion. But we do need and must return to a national truth in ultimate truth. That includes going back to the purposes that God created for each institution—family, Community, Church, and government.

I have tried in this book, to explore the four God ordained institutions and their respective God ordained purposes and how each one has abdicated those responsibilities to the federal government. I have also tried to spell out the steps for each one to return to bring their responsibilities back to its rightful position. How I have succeeded in doing this is up to the reader to decide

In the end, there is only one thing that will fix the government, the family, our communities and the church and that is what is stated in II Chronicles 7:14

> "Then if my people, who are called by my name will humble themselves and pray and seek my face and turn from their wicked ways, I will hear from heaven and will forgive their sins and restore their land. My eyes will be open and my ears opened.

So, on that note, let me offer this prayer for our country, our nation and our people:

"Our gracious Father,

You are the foundation of this world and the foundation of this great nation. We ask your forgiveness for the sin that is within us and that we have committed. We ask for your forgiveness for removing you from our land and our minds. We ask, Father, that you reestablish your spirit within our hearts and within the nation beginning with our leaders. Help us, dear Father, to turn from our wicked ways and not do the politically correct thing but the right thing according to your laws in your word and through your spirit. May our nation's leaders be filled with your spirit and lead by your divine wisdom and not the will of the majority? Oh, Lord, we place the future of this great nation in the palm of your hand.

In the name of Jesus Christ, Our Lord and Savior.

Amen

EPILOGUE

After spending a year or so writing this book, I have found that I am in a different place. Although I am still very passionate about the subject of this book, I feel a little different about the subject. As I am finishing this transcript, our world has been turned upside down with a virus pandemic and basically has made a lot of this worthless. I am now convinced that after thinking that we are in control or at least can gain control or can regain control of our country and the institutions that are the engine behind all that we do. The truth is that we are never in control and until we submit to God's control in our lives and institutions we can never fix things and as our current president says, "Make America Great Again". Until we, across our country, bow before the Lord and make Him Lord of our Land, we will not see the answers to our problems. Please read this book with the idea that God is behind everything that we can do to correct this great country. As I have prayed over the words of this book, I will pray that the reader views it with the prospective that God wants to be the head of this country and the world. Please know that my prayers are following each readers of this transcript and they will be brought to a better understanding of their creator.

I would be wrong if I did not address the person who is reading this and does not know the way back to God. I am going to share an abbreviated message as to how anyone can know God. There is 5 verses in the book of Romans that show us the way.

"For everyone has sinned; we all fall short of God's glorious standard."

This means that God requires perfection to enter his presence and His kingdom. Of course no one on earth is perfect so no one can see God. We all fall short of what is required of us.

But then in Romans 6:23, Paul says,

"For the wages of sin is death, but the free gift of God is eternal life through Christ."

In other words, God's requirement is perfection and none of us are perfect and what we have earned by that is spiritual death. But God gives us a free gift of forgiveness of sin and what has fall short of his perfection We are made perfect by Christ death of the cross./

Another truth that Paul shares with us in Romans 5:8, is this

"But God showed his great love for us by sending Christ to die for us while we were still sinners."

Then the truth Paul speaks to us is finalized in Romans 10:9,

If you openly declare that Jesus is Lord and believe in your heart that God raised him from the dead, you will be saved. For it is by believing in your heart that you are made right with God, and it is by openly declaring your faith that you are saved.

By this, Paul means that we do not have to get our lives straightened out before he accepts us but he receives us just as we are, in all of our sinfulness.

ABOUT THE AUTHOR

Pastor, teacher, administrator, business owner. Larry has been involved with education and government and politics for twenty years. He holds a BA degree from Warner Pacific University. He has pastored churches in California, Oregon, Washington and Kansas. He has also administered a private school for eight years. He is retired now and lives in Oklahoma City, Oklahoma with his wife, Paula, of 25 years. They enjoy there three granddaughters and two grandsons on a regular basis.

ADDITIONAL
RECOMMENDED
READING

Dr. Thomas Anderson, "Will the Real America Please Stand Up"

Dietrich Bonhoeffer

Glenn Beck, "Conformed"

Bible, NLT

John Dunphy, Essay

Ted Dekkar, "The Slumber of Christianity"

The Father Factor, "National Fatherhood Initiative"

Charles Finney

David Gelernter, Yale University Professor

Newt Gingrich, "Understanding Trump"

Bill Johnson, "The Way of Life"

Mark Levine, "Rediscovering Americanism"

Peter Manseau, "One Nation Under Gods"

Dr. Craig Vincent Mitchell, "The Gospel of Big Government"

David McKenna, Newsletter, "Forerunner"

Samuel Johnson

Martin Niemoller, Theologian

C. F. Potter, "Humanism, A New Religion"

James Robinson, "The Stream"

Mark Shaner, "To Russia with God's Love"

Elton Trueblood, "A Place To Stand"

Donald Trump, "Time to Get Tough"

George Washington/Alexander Hamilton

John Witherspoon

INTRERNET SITES

Lift the Vote.org

OECD/PISA.Com

END NOTES

1   Prager, Dennis, National Review
2   Potter, C.F., Humanism, A New Religion
3   Gelentner, David, Yale University Lecture
4   Fisher, Dan, "B;acl Robed Regiment, Tate Publishers, 2015
5   Robison, James, "The Stream', Worthy Publishers, 2016
6   Paine, Thomas, "American Crises"
7   Kennedy, John F., Inaugural Address 1961
8   Shaner, Mark, "To Russia With God's Love" Shaner Publishers, 2018
9   Webster, Daniel, Writingd of

Printed in the United States
By Bookmasters